WHEN THE PRESSURE'S ON

GENE A. GETZ

Regal
Books

A Division of GL Publications
Ventura, CA U.S.A.

Other good Regal reading by Gene A. Getz
Abraham: Trials and Triumphs
David: God's Man in Faith and Failure
Moses . . . Moments of Glory . . . Feet of Clay
Joshua: Defeat to Victory

Rights for publishing this book in other languages are contracted by Gospel Litera-
ture International foundation (GLINT). GLINT also provides technical help for
the adaptation, translation, and publishing of Bible study resources and books in
more than 100 languages worldwide. For further information, contact GLINT,
Post Office Box 6688, Ventura, California 93006, U.S.A., or the publisher.

Second Printing, 1985

Published by Regal Books
A Division of GL Publications
Ventura, California 93006
Printed in U.S.A.

Library of Congress Cataloging in Publication Data

Getz, Gene A.

  When the pressure's on.

  Includes bibliographical references.
    1. Elijah, the prophet. 2. Prophets—Palestine—Bibliography. 3. Bible.
O.T.—Biography. 4. Christian life—1960-
BS580.E4G47   1984   222'.50924   [B]   83-21119
ISBN 0-8307-0923-1

CONTENTS

WHY THIS STUDY?

Elijah stands out in Scripture as a man of God. He was one of the Lord's all-time greats—both in the Old and New Testaments. But what makes his story so interesting and relevant to our lives today is that he "was a man just like us." This is in fact how James describes Elijah in his New Testament letter (Jas. 5:17). His unique position in God's scheme of things did not exempt him from incredible stress, intense fear and anxiety, and crippling anger. He also experienced such severe depression that he became temporarily immobilized.

Yet, God used Elijah—and used him greatly. From day to day this Old Testament prophet discovered *renewed strength* through faith, prayer, and obedience to God's voice. This makes him an outstanding example for every twentieth-century Christian who faces the same problems—to some degree at least—as Elijah. His circumstances were certainly different, but his emotional reactions were very human. The lessons that flow from his life become biblical principles of renewal that will indeed strengthen our own commitment to God, revitalize our own prayer life, and intensify our desire to do the will of God.

RENEWAL—A BIBLICAL PERSPECTIVE

Renewal is the essence of dynamic Christianity and the basis on which Christians, both in a corporate or Body sense and as individual believers, can determine the will of God. Paul made this clear when he wrote to the Roman Christians—"be transformed by the *renewing of your mind*. Then," he continued, "you will be able to test and approve what God's will is" (Rom. 12:2). Here Paul is talking about renewal in both a personal and a corporate sense. In other words, Paul is asking these Christians as a *body* of believers to develop the mind of Christ through corporate renewal.

Personal renewal will not happen as God intended it unless it happens in the context of corporate renewal. On the other hand, corporate renewal will not happen as God intended without personal renewal. Both are necessary.

The larger circle represents "church renewal." This is the most comprehensive concept in the New Testament.

Biblical Renewal

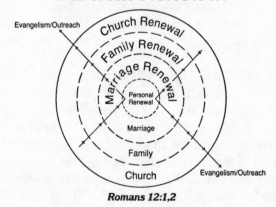

Romans 12:1,2

However, every local church is made up of smaller self-contained, but interrelated units. The *family* in Scripture emerges as the church in miniature. In turn, the family is made up of an even smaller social unit—*marriage*. The third inner circle represents *personal* renewal, which is inseparably linked to all of the other basic units. Marriage is made up of two separate individuals who become one. The family is made up of parents and children who are also to reflect the mind of Christ. And the church is made up of not only individual Christians, but couples and families.

Though all of these social units are interrelated, biblical renewal can begin within any specific social unit. But wherever it begins—in the church, families, marriages, or individuals—the process immediately touches all the other social units. And one thing is certain! All that God says is consistent and harmonious. He does not have one set of principles for the church and another set for the family, another for husbands and wives and another for individual Christians. For example, the principles God outlines for local church elders, fathers, and husbands regarding their role as leaders are interrelated and consistent. If they are not, we can be sure that we have not interpreted God's plan accurately.

Gene A. Getz

1

The Most Important Person in Life

Alongside Moses, Elijah stands out in the Old Testament as one of the most influential and powerful servants of God. In fact, C. F. Keil states, "No other prophet, either before or after, strove and worked in the idolatrous kingdom for the honor of the Lord of Sabbath with anything like the same mighty power of God as the mighty prophet Elijah."[1]

It should not surprise us that Elijah is also frequently extolled in the New Testament. It was he, along with Moses, who "appeared in glorious splendor, talking with Jesus" on the Mount of Transfiguration (Luke 9:31; see also Matt. 17:3).

There are many similarities between Elijah and his forefather, Moses. Both had unusual communication with God. Both were uniquely used by God to demonstrate His mighty power with signs and wonders and miracles. Both played a strategic role in Israel's spiritual direction.

But there's also a striking difference! We know a great deal about Moses—his parents, his birth, his early years and his preparation to be involved in Israel's destiny. By contrast, Elijah appears suddenly on the pages of Old Testament writ. He is simply identified as "Elijah the Tishbite, from Tishbe in Gilead" (1 Kings 17:1). We know nothing of his parents and his early years. We can only speculate regarding his prophetic activity prior to this moment in his life. And most Bible scholars are in agreement that we can't even pinpoint the place where he was born. Archeologists have never been able to identify with certainty the location of Tishbe, Elijah's hometown.

ELIJAH'S MISSION
1 Kings 17:1a

We cannot understand the mission God called Elijah to carry out unless we understand the historical events leading up to his confrontation with Ahab.

Historical Background

For years, Israel existed under the leadership of kings—first of King Saul, followed by David, and then David's son Solomon. God had promised Israel that if they obeyed Him, He would bless them as a nation. If they did not, then He would curse them and scatter them to the ends of the earth (Deut. 28:1-68).

This promise and warning was repeated to Solomon (1 Kings 9:1-7). But as happened so frequently among many of Israel's leaders, a good beginning had an unfortunate ending. Solomon sinned against God particularly by taking unto himself many foreign wives. Eventually he worshiped their false gods. Consequently, God dethroned Solomon and, at this juncture in Israel's history, the kingdom was split. The northern tribes continued to be called "Israel" and were initially ruled by Jeroboam. The southern tribes (Judah and Benjamin) were ruled by Rehoboam.

Both kingdoms continued to be characterized by idolatry and immorality. With few exceptions, one king after another in both nations followed in Solomon's footsteps. Ahab, the king of Israel whom Elijah confronted, was even more wicked than the kings who preceded him. This is very clear from the historical record in which we read, "Ahab son of Omri *did more evil* in the eyes of the Lord than *any of those before him*" (1 Kings 16:30).[2] And the next verse is even more specific regarding his sin. "He not only considered it *trivial* to commit the sins of Jeroboam son of Nebat, but he also married Jezebel daughter of Ethbaal king of the Sidonians, and began to serve Baal and worship him" (16:31).

Jeroboam's and Ahab's Sins

The "sins of Jeroboam" stand out boldly in Israel's history. As the first king of Israel following the division of the kingdom, he changed the central place of worship from Jerusalem to Bethel and Dan. Furthermore, he "made two golden calves" and set them up in these two locations. He then said to the people, "It is too much for you to go up to Jerusalem. Here are your gods, O Israel, who brought you up out of Egypt" (1 Kings 12:28). He also "built shrines on high places and appointed priests from all sorts of people, even though they were not Levites," a direct violation of God's commands (12:31). He not only *instructed* the children of Israel to worship false gods, but he also *modeled* the process with his own life. We read that "he instituted a festival on the fifteenth day of the eighth month, like the festival held in Judah, and offered sacrifices on the altar. This he did in Bethel, sacrificing to the calves he had made" (12:32).

Even though Jeroboam had committed a grievous sin by establishing these new places of worship and setting up false gods, his departure from God's will was not as extreme as Ahab. The "golden calves" were Egyptian symbols which were at least used to worship Jehovah. Ahab, on the other hand, took another step downward in introducing idolatry in Israel. Robert Jamieson reminds us that "Ahab effected a far worse revolution by the introduction of the heathen or Phoenician idols, Baal and Ashtaroth, and building sanctuaries to them.[3]" Though Jeroboam's actions were abominable, Ahab's were more so.

Ahab was greatly influenced in this direction by his wife, Jezebel, who was a very wicked woman. Her father was a pagan priest and his own wickedness was reflected in his daughter. Jezebel's evil reputation was so notorious that her name was used many years later by the Apostle John in the book of Revelation to illustrate the worse kind of corruption in the Church. Thus he wrote, "You tolerate that woman Jezebel, who calls herself a prophetess. By her teaching she misleads my servants into sexual immorality and the eating of food sacrificed to idols" (Rev. 2:20).

Against this historical backdrop, the nature of Elijah's mission comes into focus. We read that Ahab "did more to provoke the Lord, the God of Israel, to anger than did all the kings of Israel before him" (1 Kings 16:33). When Elijah entered the king's presence to proclaim God's judgment, he faced a wicked man who had led Israel further astray than any other leader before him.

ELIJAH'S MESSAGE
1 Kings 17:1c

Elijah's prophecy was crisp, concise and clear. Without qualification he said, "There will be neither dew nor rain in the next few years except at my word" (1 Kings 17:1c).

We have no way of knowing if Elijah prefaced these words with any other remarks or if he dialogued with Ahab following the pronouncement. Personally, I think he did not. Rather, he must have walked courageously into Ahab's presence, delivered his message without elaboration, and turned and walked out!

There is something very significant about Elijah's prophetic statement. In most instances in Scripture when a prophet was about to speak, he was introduced with the following: "The word of the Lord came to . . . " But not so in this instance! Elijah simply appeared before Ahab, the King of Israel, and made his pronouncement without this usual introduction. He simply declared, "As the Lord, the God of Israel lives, whom I serve, there will be neither dew nor rain in the next few years except at my word" (17:1).

Why didn't Elijah introduce this prophetic statement with the words, "The word of the Lord came to . . . "? Is it possible that he had no specific word from God regarding what was about to happen? You see, God had already spoken to Israel through Moses regarding what would transpire if they became guilty of idolatry. As Moses reviewed the Law before they entered the Promised Land he said, "Be careful, or you will be enticed to turn away and worship other gods and bow down to them. Then the Lord's anger will burn against you, and he will *shut the heavens so that it will not rain* and the ground will yield no produce, and you will soon perish from the good land the Lord is giving you" (Deut. 11:16-17; see also Lev. 26:19-20; and Deut. 28:23-24).

In this instance, did Elijah pray and ask God to withhold rain from the earth on the basis of his previous revelation? From what James wrote it seems this could be a possibility (Jas. 5:17). If this assumption is true, it also tells us a lot about his faith in the living God as well as what prompted Elijah to take this step.

ELIJAH'S MOTIVATION
1 Kings 17:1b

What would drive a man to speak as Elijah spoke? After all, he "was a man just like us" (Jas. 5:17). He had the same emotions, experienced the same fears, and faced the same doubts. He certainly knew in his heart before he entered Ahab's court that he *and* his message would be rejected. Furthermore, he must have known that his life was also in jeopardy.

It is clear from Elijah's overall story that his motivation was based on a God who lived and who was true to His word. He was a *man of faith*. He knew that God had already stated to Moses years before that He would "turn the rain . . . into dust and powder" (Deut. 28:24) if Israel followed false gods. And God's chosen people had done just that. Elijah had confidence that God would honor prayer that is based on God's revealed will! Before entering Ahab's presence he had "prayed earnestly that it would not rain," and as James recorded years later, "it did not rain on the land for three and a half years" (Jas. 5:17). God honored Elijah's faith!

Elijah was also a *dedicated man*. He served the living God of Abraham, Isaac, and Jacob. And he made his motivation crystal clear to Ahab. "As the Lord, the God of Israel, lives, *whom I serve* . . . " he proclaimed (1 Kings 17:1b)! With this declaration Elijah was comparing the *living* God with Ahab's gods of wood and stone.

In essence he was saying, "You serve dead gods, Ahab! I serve a God who is alive!" And unknown to Ahab, Elijah was also saying, "God Himself will prove this point!" And as we'll see, He did just that!

A NEW TESTAMENT PERSPECTIVE ON IDOLATRY

Many who became Christians in the New Testament world were also deeply involved in idol worship. This was particularly true in the Greek and Roman cultures. Though the Jews at this time were relatively free from idolatry, it was the norm in the Gentile world. For example, Luke records that Paul "was greatly distressed" in Athens when he saw "that the city was *full of idols*" (Acts 17:16). Later, this great apostle to the Gentiles created a serious riot in Ephesus because he taught "that *man-made gods* are no gods at all" (Acts 19:26). Those who made these idols and sold them in the marketplace were livid with anger because

Paul's teaching hurt their business.

The message of Jesus Christ penetrated this idolatrous environment. Those who became Christians in Thessalonica testify to this fact, for we read that they "turned to God from *idols* to serve the living and true God" (1 Thess. 1:9). In this sense, conversions were dramatic and choices clear-cut. But, as we might expect, these new Christians faced cultural problems as to what to do about idol worship, particularly as it related to the normal routines of life. For example, the Corinthians had a particular problem regarding meat which was sold in the marketplace that had already been offered to idols. In Paul's first letter to the Corinthians he helped them solve this problem (1 Cor. 8:1-13).

Idolatry, then, has been prevalent throughout history. And wherever God's true message has gone, it has confronted this evil practice head-on. Serving the living God and bowing down to dead idols are incompatible religious practices.

A TWENTIETH-CENTURY PERSPECTIVE ON IDOLATRY

It is difficult for many Christians living today, particularly in the western world, to identify with idolatry in the biblical cultures. Bowing down to idols made of wood and stone is a foreign experience to most of us. Yet, great portions of the world's population still engage in flagrant idolatry.

When my wife and I were in Hong Kong for a special ministry, we often saw people bow down to idols. Since only a small percentage of the population claims to be Christian, the majority of these people are still involved in idol worship. Their temples and shrines are filled with hundreds of images. Many homes have household gods placed outside the entrance or on god shelves. They believe these idols will bring them peace, protection, and prosperity.

We also remember visiting several church structures

while in Guatemala. Though we had often heard how many people in various parts of the world mix Christianity with their pagan religions, we were shocked to see witch doctors performing their idolatrous incantations in the main sanctuary of one of these churches.

Earlier, my wife and I had visited a cave on a mountainside just outside that particular town. The inside walls of the cave were black from the smoke of burnt offerings. The floor was strewn with the remains of animals—chicken feathers, bones, etc. Crosses were crudely sketched on the soot-covered walls. This place was well-known in the community as a "witch doctor's cave"—a place where these men engaged in ceremonial rites, praying to evil spirits and at the same time worshiping the cross of Christ.

It was shocking enough to see Christianity and paganism practiced as a unified religion in a cave on a mountainside, but to see it practiced in a church building was even more shocking. Seeing this firsthand also helped us to understand more clearly how the children of Israel blended their old idolatrous habits with the worship of the one true God. This is called *syncretism* and it is still prevalent in many parts of the world, particularly in pagan areas infiltrated by Roman Catholic missionaries.

There is a reason why this happens more frequently in Roman Catholicism than other branches of Christianity. For years statuary and images have been a prominent part of Roman Catholic worship. Though many Roman Catholics would vehemently deny bowing down to idols, it is a very natural thing for people who worship pagan idols to adopt these "Christian" symbols and integrate them into their own religious system. This, of course, happened at Mount Sinai when Israel made a golden calf to represent God. They adopted their new religion into their old idolatrous practices.

The facts are that most American Roman Catholics would be shocked at what we saw. On one occasion I was telling this story and related that I had not only seen witch doctors inside the church offering sacrifices, but the local priest was outside in the local courtyard performing mass. One person in the audience with a Roman Catholic background came up afterwards in a state of shock. He found it very difficult to believe that I was actually stating facts. And this, of course, I understand. But what I was sharing was true.

But what about those of us who would never practice this kind of idolatry? Is it possible that we too are guilty of a more subtle form of idol worship?

Do We Serve Humanistic Gods?

Paul reminded us in his Roman letter that when man departs from God's will in worship, his first step is to exchange "the glory of the immortal God for images made to look like mortal man" (Rom. 1:23). Whenever and wherever this happens, Paul continued, mankind has "exchanged the truth of God for a lie, and worshiped and served *created things* rather than the Creator" (1:25).

In our culture today, rather than worshiping *images* of people, we are more likely to worship *people*. There are many illustrations, but none are more prevalent than in the world of entertainment. When Elvis Presley died, people everywhere did incredible things to demonstrate their loyalty to a man who had probably done more than any individual at that time to corrupt the morals of our young people. And years later, people of all ages are still "worshiping" his memory—a man who died because of his drug habit.

In America we tend to glorify "people." In recent years, it seems that the more sordid their life-style, the more attention they get in the press, on radio, and on TV. Talk to the media people and they'll tell you they're giving Americans what they want!

On the religious side, Americans are often guilty of worshiping religious leaders. This is particularly true in cults with the Moonies being a classic example. However, Bible-believing Christians can also border on "pastor worship." In the minds of some people, those who lead them can become more important than the God they represent. When this happens, we are serving humanistic gods.

Do We Serve Materialistic Gods?

Jesus said, "No one can serve two masters. Either he will hate the one and love the other, or he will be devoted to the one and despise the other. You cannot serve both God and Money" (Matt. 6:24).

America is a prime environment for people from all walks of life to serve materialistic gods. In recent years, some of the highest-paid men (athletes) have gone on strike because they want more money! Some of their complaints are understandable, but it is a classic symptom of the cancerous-like disease that plagues our American culture. It is called "materialism" and the Bible calls it idolatry. Unfortunately, Christians also contract this disease. It's very contagious.

Do We Serve Sensual Gods?

Throughout history idolatry and immorality have always been closely aligned. It is not necessary to elaborate on what is happening in the American culture. More and more we are worshiping at the shrine of sex. We bow down to American sex symbols—both men and women—enjoying their flagrant immorality. We are a nation preoccupied with sensuality. This too is idolatry.

Writing to the Ephesians, Paul said, "No immoral, impure or greedy person—*such a man is an idolater*—has any inheritance in the kingdom of Christ and of God" (Eph. 5:5).

Do We Worship Relational Gods?

Ironically, at a time when marriages are breaking up,

when parents are abandoning children, and children are dishonoring their parents, there are those who have made their family relationship and friendships more important than God. Jesus said, "Anyone who loves his father or mother more than me is not worthy of me; anyone who loves his son or daughter more than me is not worthy of me; and anyone who does not take his cross and follow me is not worthy of me" (Matt. 10:37-38).

In some respects we are experiencing an overreaction regarding parent/child relationships. This is particularly true among Christians. For years, many parents neglected their children by being overly involved in religious activities. The result was rebellion and resentment towards God and the Church. But in some situations Christians have gone to the other extreme. They allow nothing—including their loyalty to God—to interfere with their relationships with family and friends. Both reactions, of course, are wrong! It is possible to put both God and family and friends in proper perspective.

A PERSONAL CHOICE

To what extent are you guilty of syncretism? There are two ways to guard against idolatry in any form.

First, you must make a choice just like Joshua of old. Standing before the children of Israel, just before they were to settle in the Promised Land, he said, "Now fear the Lord and *serve* him with all faithfulness. Throw away the gods your forefathers worshiped beyond the River and in Egypt, and *serve* the Lord. But if *serving* the Lord seems undesirable to you, then choose for yourselves this day whom you will serve, whether the gods your forefathers served beyond the River, or the gods of the Amorites, in whose land you are living."

Joshua then culminated this exhortation with a powerful, personal testimony, *"But as for me and my household,"* he said, *"we will serve the Lord"* (Joshua 24:14-15).

You too must make this choice. And when you do you must *still* be on guard against idolatry. You need to renew your commitment day by day to serve the living and true God.

Second, you must constantly evaluate your life-style in the light of God's eternal Word. The following questions can guide you: *Is there anything in my life that is consistently more important than God and His will?*

- My own personal needs
- My status and position
- My material possessions
- My recreational activities
- My job
- My leisure time
- My hobbies
- Other

If you have to answer yes to any of these questions, you should go back to Joshua's proclamation and make it your own; then from day to day you must guard against the subtle influence of twentieth-century idolatry.

Notes

1. C. F. Keil, *Commentary on the Old Testament,* vol. 3 (Grand Rapids: Wm. B. Eerdmans Publishing Co.), p. 229.

2. Hereafter all italicized words in Scripture quotations are added by the author for emphasis.

3. Robert Jamieson, *A Commentary on the Old and New Testaments,* vol. 2 (Grand Rapids: Wm B. Eerdmans Publishing Co., 1948), p. 348.

Pray.

2

A Place to Hide

Elijah in Ch 1 has told Ahab if God want He could stop Rain until Elijah said it would - Repent Ahab for your idols + serve the one + the live God

We're not told specifically what Ahab's immediate or subsequent reactions were when Elijah marched into his court and announced that there was going to be a serious drought because of his idolatrous actions. But we can speculate! If the king initially laughed at this eccentric old prophet and his daring feat, his unwillingness to take Elijah seriously soon changed when it stopped raining. It doesn't take long for people to get nervous when both their food and water supply begin to run low. When the productive and fruitful valleys in Israel began to turn into dust bowls, God had Ahab's attention.

Rather than turning from his sins and leading Israel to forsake their idols and to worship Jehovah, Ahab focused his frustration on Elijah. He put out an all-points alert to try and bring this troublemaker into custody, revealing the extent to which he had forsaken the God of his forefathers. Either he did not realize what he was doing in trying to capture this representative of the living God or he refused to

believe what he knew was true. To wage war on Elijah was
to wage war on the Creator of the Universe. Ahab would
not accept the fact that for him, and the people of Israel, this
was ultimately a no-win situation.

GOD'S PROTECTION
1 Kings 17:2-3

When Elijah's life was in danger because of Ahab's
determination to find him, "the word of the Lord came to
Elijah" (1 Kings 17:2). We're also told specifically what
God said. "Leave here, turn eastward and hide in the Kerith
Ravine, east of the Jordan" (1 Kings 17:3).

As with Tishbe, Elijah's birthplace, there's no way to
determine the exact location of this "hiding place." Bible
commentators agree only on one thing—it could have been
one of many places, since there were numerous ravines in
this general area. This, of course, is why it was a safe place
for Elijah.

Again and again in Scripture, particularly throughout
the Old Testament, we encounter this basic scenario. God
often protected His servants from their enemies when they
took a stand against idolatry.

This is demonstrated dramatically in the book of Daniel.
On one occasion Daniel's three friends—Shadrach,
Meshach and Abednego—refused to bow down to a huge
idol constructed by King Nebuchadnezzar. They defied an
order issued by the king himself, knowing that he had commanded that anyone who did "*not* fall down and worship"
the huge, ninety-foot image would "immediately be thrown
into a blazing furnace" (Dan. 3:6).

When Nebuchadnezzar received word that these three
men, his faithful servants, had refused to bow down to the
idol, he was furious. And because they were his servants,
he issued a summons that they appear before him to explain
their defiance.

"Is it true, Shadrach, Meshach and Abednego," the king

asked, "that you do not serve my gods or worship the image of gold I have set up?" (3:14).

Without wavering these men responded, "O Nebuchadnezzar, we do not need to defend ourselves before you in this matter. If we are thrown into the blazing furnace, the God we serve is able to save us from it, and he will rescue us from your hand, O king" (3:16-17).

God *did* choose to deliver these men. In his anger the king had the furnace heated seven times hotter than usual. In fact, it was so hot that the men who threw Shadrach, Meshach, and Abednego into the blazing inferno were themselves killed.

But lo and behold, when the king looked into the furnace he saw "four men walking around in the fire, unbound and unharmed." "Look!" he shouted. "The fourth looks like a son of the gods" (3:25).

Without knowing it, Nebuchadnezzar was looking not at a son of the gods but at the *Son of God!* This was probably an Old Testament appearance of Jesus Christ.

God miraculously protected these men who stood so firmly against idolatry. And later the Lord did the same for Daniel. A decree had been issued by King Darius that, for a certain period of time, if anyone prayed to any god or man rather than to him, he would be thrown into a den of lions (6:7). Daniel ignored this decree and continued his practice of getting down on his knees three times a day and praying to the living God. When this was reported to the king, he had Daniel thrown into the lions' den. But once again we see God's miraculous protection. The Lord sent an angel (probably Jesus Christ Himself) who "shut the mouths of the lions" (6:22) and Daniel was released unharmed.

Just so, God protected Elijah who in essence many years earlier had taken the same stand as Daniel and his three friends. Who knows? Perhaps it was Elijah's sterling example that gave these men courage to refuse to worship false gods.

GOD'S PROVISION
1 Kings 17:4-6

God not only protected Elijah from Ahab, but also provided for His servant's material needs. Elijah too was a victim of the drought he had asked God to bring on Israel. Consequently, God led him to a place where he could drink water from a brook. But in addition to this *natural* provision, the Lord *supernaturally* provided Elijah with food. "I have ordered the ravens to feed you there," God said (1 Kings 17:4).

Why did God choose birds to provide Elijah with food? And why ravens, especially since they were classified by God as unclean birds that should never be eaten (Lev. 11:13-15; Deut. 14:11-14)? There are several possible explanations.

God Was Still in Control

God was certainly reassuring Elijah that *He* had not forsaken him. Since Elijah was a "man just like us" he would be tempted to doubt God's involvement in his life when the pressure was on—especially this kind of pressure.

Isaiah once wrote that God could "command the clouds" and they would not yield rain (Isa. 5:6). Indeed this is what He had done in response to Elijah's prayer. And there in the wilderness, hiding from Ahab, God told His servant He would command the ravens to feed him both morning and evening. Daily, when the sun arose and when it set in the evening, the ravens served as a constant reminder that God was still in control of nature. Even animals were subject to His direction.

God Was Concerned About Elijah's Deepest Needs

Why did God not provide Elijah with manna as He had done for the children of Israel years before as they wandered in the wilderness? God was also sensitive to Elijah's emotional needs—his loneliness. Rather than leaving him alone in a wilderness place, surrounded with trees, bushes, and shrubs that were themselves beginning to reflect a look of death for lack of moisture, God in His grace provided His servant daily a touch with *life*. How Elijah must have looked forward to seeing those ravens arrive each morning and evening!

God Was Assuring Elijah He Can Use Anything and Anyone

The fact that ravens were considered "unclean" birds would be a regular reminder that the Lord can even use unclean vessels to accomplish His tasks. Should Elijah be tempted to doubt his worthiness to be involved in such a dramatic plan, the ravens would remind him regularly that God can use a man even though he feels unequal to the task.

HE CAN USE US TODAY

God Added a "Special Touch"

Finally, note that the Lord provided Elijah with *both* "bread and meat." He could have provided him with bread *or* just meat. Elijah could have survived on either. But God provided him with *both*—a balanced diet. In other words, God added that "something extra" to encourage him in the midst of a very difficult experience.

Whatever the reasons God had for sending ravens to feed Elijah, it seems clear that He met Elijah's needs not only physically but psychologically and spiritually. It is an unusual reminder that God cares about His children, especially those who are serving Him in special ways.

TIME of Preparation

GOD'S PREPARATION

There is another factor that relates to Elijah's experience in this wilderness place. Almost every person whom God has used to accomplish a special task has gone through a time of preparation. And often that preparation has involved isolation, rejection, and loneliness.

How true this was of Moses! He spent forty years on the backside of the desert after his first forty years in Egypt. Unknown to him at that time, God was preparing him for the greatest task ever to face a human being—leading the children of Israel out of Egypt. Without that preparation, Moses would not have been ready for the difficulties he would face.

Years later, Joseph spent a number of years in an Egyptian prison before he was promoted to the position of prime minister in the same country. Without those prison experiences and the rejection involved, he would not have been ready for the task God designed for him.

The Apostle Paul, following his conversion to Christ, spent three years in obscurity in Arabia. While he was there God was preparing him to become a great missionary to the Gentile world. Without that preparation, he would not have been ready.

Even Jesus Christ, the Son of God and Saviour of the world, spent years in obscurity before entering a public ministry. His forty days in the wilderness was a final touch in preparation to face the lonely road which lay ahead and which eventuated in the cross.

It should not surprise us then, that God was doing something special in Elijah's life in preparing him for what lay ahead. And in future chapters we'll see why Elijah needed that preparation.

WHAT ABOUT YOU AND ME?

Some of God's greatest lessons for all of us emerge from the study of the lives and experiences of Old Testament characters. Elijah is no exception. Though he was a great prophet of God, he was still "a man just like us."

In making these applications, however, we must be careful to consider what God says in both the Old and New Testaments regarding His will.

Some Cautions

Elijah was a special person with a special calling to accomplish a special mission. Consequently, it is dangerous to generalize to our own experience in every particular. For example, God often spoke *directly* to Elijah and told him what to do. This is why he was an Old Testament prophet in the true sense of that word. He often became God's mouthpiece to Israel.

There are some people who believe God speaks to them today just like He did to Elijah. God could, of course, for He can do anything He wants to do. But in the most part it seems He has chosen not to. Rather, once He spoke *through* His apostles and prophets and gave us the holy Scriptures, He has chosen to use that revealed Word to communicate His will. Generally speaking, the Scriptures give us everything we need to know to be able to determine His will for our lives.

The need to be cautious in this matter was impressed upon my mind one day when a lady approached me regarding her husband. He was not a Christian and wanted nothing to do with her spiritual conviction, her church, or her Lord. He had secured an attorney and was trying to have her evicted from the home. Previously she had also secured an attorney, but released him from the case because she believed God had "told her" that her husband was going to become a Christian, that he was going to accept her spiritual convictions, and was going to go with her and her family to serve as missionaries on the foreign mission field. However she was concerned because it was not working out the way God had "told her" it would.

First let me emphasize that this lady was not mentally or emotionally ill. She simply had been taught that God speaks to Christians today just as He did to Elijah. As with so many people who have been taught this, she had sincerely simulated an historical and real spiritual experience with some kind of subjective psychological experience. And she was headed into a serious problem that would leave her more disillusioned than before.

"I'm not sure it was God speaking to you," I told her after listening to her story.

"You aren't?" she said. "Was it Satan then?" reflecting another confused view regarding supernatural communications.

"No, I don't believe it was Satan," I replied.

"Was it just me?" she asked.

"Yes, I believe it was probably just you—your desire, your hope for the future," I told her.

In this case, as in so many cases, this woman was "speaking to herself." Her deep desires became internal verbal signals. And she believed it was God speaking to her through her mind.

Later in the conversation she indicated that she felt that God had also given her a similar message through some verses of Scripture in the book of Acts. After discussing the literal context of that Scripture, she saw that she was misusing the Word of God.

You can see how dangerous it can be either to believe that God is speaking *directly* through our mental and psychological apparatus, or to believe that God is speaking through Scripture that has been taken out of context. There are people who very sincerely get out of God's will because they listen to these "voices" from within. The voice Elijah heard was not from within. It was external. It was *from God*.

The Scriptures are also from God. They can be trusted. But we must make sure that we interpret Scripture correctly. If we are not cautious we can even use the Scriptures subjectively and make them say anything *we* want them to say. With this in mind, let's see how we *can* discern the will of God through the whole of Scriptures.

Some Challenges

What about God's protection and provisions for us today? When we study the whole of Scripture we discover that God has promised to be with us at all times. However, He has never promised that He will *always deliver us* from problems, difficulties, or even death. But He has promised to sustain us and never to leave our side.

Even Shadrach, Meshach, and Abednego recognized this distinction. First, they made it clear to King Nebuchadnezzar that the God they served *was able* to protect them from death—even a fiery furnace. And, of course, God did. But they also knew He might not! And they made it clear to the king that if God chose to take them to heaven, they would still not serve false gods (Dan. 3:17-18).

The Apostle Paul also understood this distinction. Before he died, probably executed by the evil Roman emperor, Nero, he wrote these words to Timothy: "At my first defense, no one came to my support, but everyone deserted me. May it not be held against them. But the Lord stood at my side and gave me strength, so that through me the message might be fully proclaimed and all the Gentiles might hear it. And I was delivered from the lion's mouth. The Lord will rescue me from every evil attack and will bring me safely to his heavenly kingdom. To Him be glory for ever and ever. Amen (2 Tim. 4:16-18).

What does Paul mean? He knew God would never forsake him. Whether he lived or died he knew God would enable him to face his persecutors triumphantly. His deliverance would come—either to remain on this earth to fulfill God's will or to be set free from his earthly body and enjoy the splendors of heaven. In Paul's mind he would be free either way. He sensed God's divine protection. This is what he meant when he wrote to the Philippians from a Roman prison and said, "I eagerly expect and hope that I will in no way be ashamed, but will have sufficient courage so that now as always Christ will be exalted in my body, whether by life *or* by death. For to me, to live is Christ and to die is gain (Phil. 1:20-21).

The Scriptures teach that this kind of protection is *always* available to a believer. Jesus Christ will never leave us or forsake us. And Christians through the centuries who have faced this kind of persecution have demonstrated with their lives this reality. Some have lived to talk about it, such as Kefa Sempangi.

Kefa founded and pastored the fourteen-thousand-member Redeemed Church of Uganda, which became a target of Idi Amin's intense persecution in 1973. Thousands of people throughout Uganda were exterminated by Amin's Nubian assassins. However, God chose to miraculously deliver Kefa and his family from death. Kefa describes one of those moments in his book *A Distant Grief*. It was Easter Sunday and Kefa had preached most of the day to thousands who had gathered from miles around. At the end of the day, as the sun was going down, he closed the service. And then it happened! He writes:

> I greeted several more friends and then left for the vestry to change my clothes, hoping to have a few minutes alone in prayer. I had to push my way through the crowd and when I finally arrived at the house I was exhausted. I was too tired to notice the men behind me until they had closed the door.
>
> There were five of them. They stood between me and the door, pointing their rifles at my face. Their own faces were scarred with the distinctive tribal cuttings of the Kakwa tribe. They were dressed casually in flowered shirts and bell-bottom pants, and wore sunglasses. Although I had never seen any of them before, I recognized them immediately. They were the secret police of the State Research Bureau—Amin's Nubian assassins.

For a long moment no one said anything. Then the tallest man, obviously the leader, spoke. "We are going to kill you," he said. "If you have something to say, say it before you die." He spoke quietly but his face was twisted with hatred.

I could only stare at him. For a sickening moment I felt the full weight of his rage. We had never met before but his deepest desire was to tear me to pieces. My mouth felt heavy and my limbs began to shake. Everything left my control. *They will not need to kill me,* I thought to myself. *I am just going to fall over. I am going to fall over dead and I will never see my family again.* I thought of Penina home alone with Damali. What would happen to them when I was gone?

From far away I heard a voice, and I was astonished to realize it was my own. "I do not need to plead my own cause," I heard myself saying. "I am a dead man already. My life is dead and hidden in Christ. It is your lives that are in danger, you are dead in your sins. I will pray to God that after you have killed me, He will spare you from eternal destruction."

The tall one took a step towards me and then stopped. In an instant, his face was changed. His hatred had turned to curiosity. He lowered his gun and motioned to the others to do the same. They stared at him in amazement but they took their guns from my face.

Then the tall one spoke again. "Will you pray for us now?" he asked.

I thought my ears were playing a trick. I looked at him and then at the others. My mind was completely paralyzed. The tall one repeated his question more loudly, and I could see that he was becoming impatient.

"Yes, I will pray for you," I answered. My voice

sounded bolder even to myself. "I will pray to the Father in heaven. Please bow your heads and close your eyes."

The tall one motioned to the others again, and together the five of them lowered their heads. I bowed my own head, but I kept my eyes open. The Nubian's request seemed to me a strange trick. Any minute, I thought to myself, my life will end. I did not want to die with my eyes closed.

"Father in heaven," I prayed, "you who have forgiven men in the past, forgive these men also. Do not let them perish in their sins but bring them unto yourself."

It was a simple prayer, prayed in deep fear. But God looked beyond my fears and when I lifted my head, the men standing in front of me were not the same men who had followed me into the vestry. Something had changed in their faces.

It was the tall one who spoke first. His voice was bold but there was no contempt in his words. "You have helped us," he said, "and we will help you. We will speak to the rest of our company and they will leave you alone. Do not fear for your life. It is in our hands and you will be protected."

I was too astonished to reply. The tall one only motioned for the others to leave. He himself stepped to the doorway and then he turned to speak one last time. "I saw widows and orphans in the congregation," he said. "I saw them singing and giving praise. Why are they happy when death is so near?"

It was still difficult to speak but I answered him. "Because they are loved by God. He has given them life, and will give life to those they loved, because they died in Him."

His question seemed strange to me, but he did not stay to explain. He only shook his head in perplexity and walked out the door.[1]

Note

1. F. Kefa Sempangi, *A Distant Grief* (Ventura, CA: Regal Books, 1979), pp. 119-121.

IN CONCLUSION GOD TODAY
Speaks through his Written Word.
I am Realizing More how important
it is for me to Read.
and ~~this~~ therfore understand what God
wants for me and what he says
to me through his Scriptures

Pray.

3

Experiencing God's Faithfulness

Elijah had already experienced God's faithful care in "the Kerith Ravine." There Elijah drank from a brook and every morning and evening ate bread and meat delivered by ravens. But this man of God was to experience even more of God's care and concern for him.

GOD'S FAITHFULNESS WHEN THE BROOK DRIED UP
1 Kings 17:7-13

How long Elijah lived in the ravine we don't know. Some Bible interpreters believe it was at least a year—maybe longer. Nevertheless, Elijah's anxiety level must have risen as the drought continued and the stream of water eventually became a mere trickle. Eventually, "the brook dried up" altogether (1 Kings 17:7).

All during this period of isolation from the outside world, Elijah never missed a meal. The ravens faithfully carried out God's directive. Imagine what was happening to

Elijah's faith as the water level in that brook got lower and lower. The Lord could have brought water out of the rocks as He did for Israel years before as they traveled through the wilderness. But to build faith on an historical event, especially when it happened to someone else, is difficult for any person, even a prophet of God. Again we must remember James's words, "Elijah was a man just like us." Even though our needs are being met in one or several areas, it's the area where our needs are *not* being met that causes our greatest frustration and doubt. For Elijah, his need for water would certainly tend to overshadow others. Considering the circumstances, his tendency to panic would certainly be a normal reaction, especially since each day the water level lowered was a constant reminder that time was running out.

Imagine too the temptation Elijah must have faced to want to reverse God's judgment. After all, it was his prayers that caused the Lord to shut the windows of heaven and eventually it would be his prayers that would once again bring rain. His own fears and needs must have tempted him to speed up the process.

When Did God Speak to Elijah?

At the last moment—and evidently not before—"the word of the Lord" came to Elijah, directing him away from Kerith. "Go at once to Zarephath of Sidon and stay there," God said. "I have commanded a widow in that place to supply you with food" (17:8-9).

The command to "go *at once*" underscores the urgency of the situation. It should not surprise us that Elijah wasted no time obeying. And sure enough, when he arrived at Zarephath, he met a widow at the gate gathering sticks.

Why a Poor Widow?

It's fascinating that God chose a poor widow to meet Elijah's needs—a widow who had only enough food for a final meal. Why did God choose this lonely person who herself was destitute and in desperate need? There are probably several reasons which affected the widow herself, her son, as well as Elijah—*and us!* There are some powerful lessons in this story even for us who live in an entirely different culture. The Lord, as He did so often, can minister in a special way to a variety of people with various needs with a single event. Elijah's encounter with the widow at Zarephath certainly illustrates this point.

First, God is concerned when His children are in need. God chose this widow because she and her son were in need. Her food supply was almost depleted. When Elijah asked her for a drink of water and some bread, she replied, "I don't have any bread—only a handful of flour in a jar and a little oil in a jug. I am gathering a few sticks to take home and make a meal for myself and my son, that we may eat it—and die" (17:12).

This was not a tongue-in-cheek comment. This is why Elijah responded, "Don't be afraid" (17:13)! Fear was written all over her face in what must have been a frail body, reflecting her lack of nourishment. For days she must have cautiously limited the intake of food for both her son and herself.

Few of us have ever experienced being down to our last meal for our family, with no hope of what to do next. And certainly few of us have been in a situation where we have been asked to give what little we have left to someone else. Just facing the prospect of starvation over a period of time would be enough to create deep fear and anxiety. And now to be asked to share what she had left with a stranger must have left her with feelings beyond our imagination.

One reason, then, that God sent Elijah to this poor widow is that she was a believer in deep need. The Lord knew her food supply was almost gone. Perhaps she had been praying and asking God for help.

Second, God cares about His children no matter what their status in life. This widow lived not among the children of Israel but in Sidon, a Gentile community. In fact, it was the very territory in which Jezebel, Ahab's wicked wife, lived before she married the king of Israel. Evidently the widow was a Gentile believer and this is a *second* reason why God chose this widow. She illustrates God's concern for all people everywhere.

Wherever people believe on Him and trust Him, no matter who they are or what their background and resources, He is ready to reveal His mercy. He honors faith, as we see illustrated in the life of another Gentile woman many years later who lived in the same area as this widow at Zarephath. She came to Jesus one day, asking that He might heal her daughter who was demon possessed. Interestingly, Jesus did not respond, testing her faith. The disciples picked up on His silence—probably as Jesus had planned—and tried to send her away. At this stage in their growth and development they were not known for their lack of prejudice toward Gentiles.

Jesus then responded to this woman by telling her that He had been "sent only to the lost sheep of Israel" (Matt. 15:24). On hearing this, Jesus' disciples must have swollen with pride. But the woman humbled herself and knelt before Jesus, pleading for mercy and help.

Jesus replied again, "It is not right to take the children's bread and toss it to their dogs" (15:26). Though it appears all along that Jesus was speaking to the woman only, He was actually speaking more directly to His disciples. In fact, He was probably taking the very words out of their minds, for they indeed were terribly prejudiced towards Gentiles. In this sense He was testing their faith and at the same time teaching His disciples a powerful lesson.

In view of these words from Christ, the woman's response reflected great faith, wisdom and humility. "Yes, Lord," she said, "but even the dogs eat the crumbs that fall from their masters' table" (15:27).

These words from a Gentile woman were in themselves

a powerful message to Jesus' disciples. But Jesus, knowing this moment was coming, put the finishing touches on her message with these words, "Woman, you have great faith! Your request is granted." At that very moment He healed her daughter (Matt. 15:28). And once again Jesus taught two lessons simultaneously—one to a Gentile woman who needed to develop her faith, and another to a group of disciples who needed to know that some Gentiles actually had more faith than they did.

In some respects, the widow of Zarephath is an Old Testament prelude to this New Testament story. Elijah was sent to the Gentile woman for help. She herself was in great need, and since she worshiped the true God, the Lord not only was going to use her to meet a deep need in her own life, but also to meet a special need in Elijah's life. And this leads us to a another reason God chose this widow.

GOD'S FAITHFULNESS WHEN THE "JAR" AND "JUG" WERE EMPTY
1 Kings 17:11-16

Elijah had a gigantic task ahead of him and he needed reassurance that God was still in control; therefore, *God was reassuring Elijah of His continual presence and power.*

For at least a year the Lord had commanded the ravens to feed Elijah. And now He prepared a widow lady to do the same thing. The message is clear. God does not need great and mighty subjects to be His ministers. If He can use birds as well as a poor widow, He can certainly use anything and anyone! Elijah needed that continual reassurance.

Furthermore, God was teaching Elijah to continue to rely upon Him. You see, if God had sent Elijah to someone who had a great supply of food, He may have been tempted to stop praying and trusting God. How quickly that happens when we have no deep need.

It seems at that moment that Elijah knew God was going to take care of all of them—the widow, her son and himself. Consequently he said, "Go home and do as you have said. But first make a small cake of bread for me from what you have and bring it to me, and then make something for yourself and your son. For this is what the Lord, the God of Israel says: 'The jar of flour will not be used up and the jug of oil will not run dry until the day the Lord gives rain on the land' " (1 Kings 17:13-14).

God honored the widow woman's faith and obedience. "She went away and did as Elijah had told her." And "there was food *every day* for Elijah and for the woman and her family. For the jar of flour was not used up and the jug of oil did not run dry, in keeping with the word of the Lord spoken by Elijah" (17:15-16).

Note that God supplied "food *every day*." There was never more than they needed or less than they needed. In this sense, the lesson was greater for Elijah than for the woman. All during this period of waiting, God kept reassuring Elijah of His power. The appearance of the ravens with food every morning and evening were a constant reminder. And now the jar and jug were never empty. Elijah needed that constant reminder of God's faithfulness.

Furthermore, Elijah was learning that faith must be constant. Had the Lord miraculously given him a barrel of flour and a keg of oil, the need to keep trusting God would not have been as great. Elijah, like all of us, needed to learn to trust God constantly.

IS THERE ANYTHING IN THIS STORY FOR TWENTIETH-CENTURY CHRISTIANS?

God is concerned about all people. It doesn't matter who you are, your age, your sex, your marital state, your economic situation, or your ethnic background. You can be Jew or Gentile, black or white, rich or poor. It doesn't matter. God loves you! He demonstrates that again and again in Scripture. The widow of Zarephath illustrates this point specifically.

Though Jesus was a Jew and came to His own people first, He did so to launch a mission to the whole world. "You will be my witnesses," Jesus said, "in Jerusalem, and in all Judea and Samaria, and to the ends of the earth" (Acts 1:8).

God honors those who put others first, particularly when we share material possessions in a sacrificial way. The widow of Zarephath also illustrates this point. Think how difficult it was for her to take all that she had to eat and share it with Elijah first. That would be difficult for us all.

Many years later, Jesus illustrates this point with another poor widow. On one occasion Jesus was watching people in the Temple as they filed by to put their gifts in a special offering box. Using today's language, one person put in $10, another $100 and someone else $1,000. But, we read that "He also saw a poor widow put in two very small copper coins."

Jesus was deeply moved at what He saw, and He used it as a point of teaching. "I tell you the truth," He said, "this poor widow has put in more than all the others. All these people gave their gifts out of their wealth; but she out of her poverty put in all she had to live on" (Luke 21:1-4).

Is Jesus saying that poor people ought to give all they have? If we believe this, we miss the point completely. The message was for those who had more than she did. He was saying that she gave more than all the rest. And if others were to give sacrificially, they would have to give a lot more of what they had left over.

Isn't it amazing how often giving and sharing appear in the Bible? Why does God emphasize it so frequently? I think Dr. Charles Ryrie answers this question very succinctly in his book *Balancing the Christian Life:*

To be sure, a vital spiritual life is related to fellowship with the Lord in His word and prayer and to service for the Lord in His work. But our love for God may be proved by something that is a major part of everyone's life, and that is our use of money. How we use our money demonstrates the reality of our love for God. In some ways it proves our love more conclusively than depth of knowledge, length of prayers or prominence of service. These things can be feigned, but the use of our possessions shows us up for what we actually are.[1]

God delights in taking what we have, as inadequate as it may seem—our talents, our time, our material resources—*and multiplying their effectiveness.*

For the widow, the jar of meal was constantly replenished and the jug of oil never ran dry. This, of course, was a dramatic miracle. It had to be if she and her son—and Elijah—were going to survive.

Can God work this kind of miracle for us today? We must remember that this supernatural provision continued *only* until it began to rain again (1 Kings 17:14). When the natural means were there, God expected people to provide for themselves from the natural resources that He had already provided.

However, for all of us there comes a time when we must turn to God for divine intervention. When we trust Him day by day and do all that we can do with the resources that He has given us, and yet we cannot meet our needs, He must go beyond our natural capabilities. Furthermore, God can do this, just as He did it in this Old Testament story.

How often this happened to Nehemiah and to the children of Israel when they were building the walls of Jerusalem! They worked hard, doing everything they could do! They planned, organized and at times worked around the clock. But there were also times when they had to face the fact that they needed God's supernatural intervention. Though they had been praying and trusting God all along, they needed at times to stop and say, "Lord, without your miraculous intervention we can't go on. We cannot succeed." And God again and again provided that miracle.

And this leads us to our final lesson.

At times the Lord keeps us on the edge of uncertainty to develop our faith and trust in Him. Had the Lord led Elijah from the ravine of Kerith to a fruitful plantation flowing with milk and honey, Elijah would certainly have enjoyed it. But he would have followed his human tendency that is in us all to get sidetracked from the mission God had for him. Remember, he "was a man just like us." And God knew the mission that lay ahead was going to call for some spiritual faith and emotional energy far beyond anything he had ever experienced before.

This is difficult for any Christian. And yet, when everything is going smoothly, when we have all we need, and when the road is clear before us, we tend to over-rely on our wisdom, our abilities and our own energy. Consequently, God often provides opportunities for us to grow in our faith in order to be even more effective in our work for Him.

This is particularly necessary for those of us who in many respects live in a "land flowing with milk and honey." Opportunities are everywhere! Why pray? Why trust God? Why rely on Him when we can make our way in life, even as Christians?

The effects of culture on us were indelibly impressed on my mind when I read the story told by Kefa Sempangi. After he and his wife and family were miraculously delivered from certain death if he had stayed in Uganda, they came to the United States to study. Just a few months after he was in the United States, a change began to take place in his life. He tells about that change with the following words:

> Our first semester passed quickly. Penina gave birth to our son, Dawudi Babumba. In the fall I returned to my studies. It was then, in my second year, that I noticed the change that had come into my

life. In Uganda, Penina and I read the Bible for hope and life. We read to hear God's promises, to hear His commands and obey them. There had been no time for argument, no time for religious discrepancies or doubts.

Now, in the security of a new life and with the reality of death fading from my mind, I found myself reading Scripture to analyze texts and to speculate about meaning. I came to enjoy abstract discussions with my fellow students and, while these discussions were intellectually refreshing, it wasn't long before our fellowship revolved around ideas rather than the work of God in our lives. It was not the blood of Christ that gave us unity, but our agreement on doctrinal issues. We came together not for confession and forgiveness but for debate.

The biggest change came to my prayer life. In Uganda I had prayed with a deep sense of urgency. I refused to leave my knees until I was certain I had been in the presence of the resurrected Christ. It was not just the gift I needed. I needed to see the Giver. I needed to know that the God of orphans and widows, the God of the helpless, heard my prayers. Now, after a year in Philadelphia, the urgency was gone. When I prayed publicly I was more concerned to be theologically correct than to be in God's presence. Even in private my prayers were no longer the helpless cries of a child. They were spiritual tranquilizers, thoughts that made no contact with anything outside themselves. More and more I found myself coming to God with vague requests for gifts I did not expect.

One night I said my prayers in a routine fashion and was about to rise from my knees when I heard the convicting voice of the Holy Spirit.

"Kefa, who were you praying for? What is it you wanted? I used to hear the names of children in your prayers, the names of friends and relatives . . . . Now you pray for 'the orphans,' for 'the church' and your 'fellow-refugees.' Which refugees, Kefa? Which believers? Which orphans? Who are these people and what is it you want for them?"

It was a sharp rebuke. As I fell again to my knees and asked forgiveness for my sin of unbelief, I knew that it was not just my prayers that had suffered. It was not just a bad memory that had caused names to vanish from my mind and turned those closest to me into abstractions. God Himself had become a distant figure. He had become a subject of debate, an abstract category. I no longer prayed to Him as a living Father, but as an impersonal being who did not mind my inattention and unbelief.

From that night on, my prayers became specific. I prayed for real people, with real needs. And it was not long before, once again, these needs became the means by which I came face to face with the living God.[2]

Let it be said in conclusion that God does not want us to live in a constant state of tension. Even Elijah could not handle that. God also wants us to enjoy the good things of life. We all need relief from pressures. Even Jesus needed that as well as His disciples, and thus He said to them one day, "Come with me by yourselves to a quiet place and get some rest" (Mark 6:31). And Paul said as he wrote to the Philippians "I know what it is to be in need, and I know what it is to have plenty. I have learned the secret of being content in any and every situation, whether well fed or hungry, whether living in plenty or in want." And then he added, "I can do everything through him who gives me strength" (Phil. 4:12-13).

PERSONAL LIFE RESPONSE

1. Do I really believe that God cares for me? He does! Will I accept that fact? Will I believe it?

2. To what extent am I thinking of others' needs before I think of my own? How is this reflected in my stewardship of time, my material resources and my abilities?

3. Do I believe God can take what I have and multiply it? What evidence do I have that I believe this?

4. How strong is my faith? How much do I really rely upon God? Is it possible that some of my uncertainties at the present time are ordered by the Lord to develop my spiritual life? Am I resisting God or am I submitting to Him in order to learn more about His plan for my life?

Notes

1. Charles Ryrie, *Balancing the Christian Life* (Chicago: Moody Press, 1969), p. 84.
2. F. Kefa Sempangi, *A Distant Grief* (Ventura, CA: Regal Books, 1979), pp. 179,180.

4

Learning to Pray

God's plan for Elijah was on schedule. When Elijah feared for his life, God told him where to hide. When there was no food, God used the ravens to feed him. When the brook dried up, God sent him to a widow in Sidon. And when Elijah discovered she had no food left to share, God provided enough oil and meal each day so the widow, her son, and Elijah could survive. As this man of God faced what appeared to be one insurmountable problem after another, God faithfully cared for His servant.

At times Elijah must have reflected back and wondered about his own sanity in taking on the king of Israel in the name of His God. At times he must have gone through periods of deep doubt wondering whether God was still in control. But with each difficulty God was faithful in caring for Elijah. In each instance this man of God did not know immediately how and when God was going to take care of him, but the Lord never ceased to meet his needs.

As we've noted all along, God was preparing Elijah for

an even greater task. In God's scheme of things he had to go through another test before he was prepared to encounter Ahab and his false prophets face to face. It happened in the widow's home.

A FAMILY CRISIS
1 Kings 17:17-18

We read that "some time later the son of the woman who owned the house became ill" (17:17). Again we do not know what specific time period is involved. However, from the overall time references in Elijah's story we can conclude it must have been several months. Although the widow's oil jug and her meal jar never ran empty, enabling them to make bread each day, it did not keep sickness away from her home. Her son "became ill."

It was not a sudden attack that left him near death. Rather the boy's health deteriorated over a period of time. He grew "worse and worse, and finally stopped breathing" (17:17).

Though the biblical text reports this tragic event very succinctly, it allows room for a lot of realistic speculation as to what happened. When the boy finally "stopped breathing," the widow openly expressed her deep feelings of anxiety and distress to Elijah. "What do you have against me, man of God? Did you come to remind me of my sin and kill my son?" (17:18)

Imagine what must have happened. For days, or perhaps weeks, the boy's illness worsened. The first day or two the widow no doubt showed little concern—nor did Elijah. After all, the oil and meal were always there! And all of us have faced periods of illness that come and go.

But as the days passed, it became evident this was no ordinary illness. The boy was not recovering. His mother's casual concern turned to intense fear—and penetrating introspection. In times like these, it is natural to begin to ask the question "Why?" Human tragedy is always sobering—especially when it involves death.

The Widow's Response

The widow's reactions were predictable. She looked for a reason for what was happening and her thoughts turned inward. By now she had come to know Elijah. He was no ordinary man. He was different from other men she had known. Her pagan friends were licentious and sinful. No doubt she had lived the same sinful life-style. But for several months now, she had lived in the same house with a man who *was* different. Not once had he tried to use her for selfish reasons. And even if she had made herself available, he would have discussed with her the eternal laws of God that had been revealed to Israel at Sinai. She'd come to know Elijah as a "man of God." And the more she came to know him—what he believed and how he lived, and what his mission in life really was—the more cognizant she became of her own sins. And thus she said to Elijah, "What do you have against me, *man of God?* Did you come to *remind me of my sin* and kill my son?"

As her son lay dying, this woman's introspection focused on her former life-style. Was it her sin that was causing her son's illness? Was it God's judgment? Had Elijah come to reveal her sinful ways and then to bring God's judgment upon her? Was this why her son lay dying?

On the one hand, the widow was tempted to do what many people do when tragedy strikes. Their view of God often leads them to wonder if God is punishing them for some sin either in their past life or in the present. Lingering guilt has ways of causing this paranoia. She had not yet learned that God does not hold grudges. Though on rare occasions God had punished sin in this way—as He did with David for his terrible sin of adultery and murder—it is not the normal way God works. That is especially true when it comes to our past sins. And even when we are committing sins in the present, He is very long-suffering. Even in David's case, when God's law specifically declared that he should die for taking life, God let him live.

On the other hand, this widow knew that it did not seem logical for Elijah to save both her and her son from starvation, only to turn around and take his life once she became aware of her sins. From this vantage point we can certainly understand her questions, her fears, and her confusion.

Elijah's Response

Elijah too was deeply troubled and touched. By now he had come to know this little family well. After a year of loneliness in the ravine of Kerith, you can imagine how refreshing it had been for Elijah to once again spend his days with people. His heart was touched deeply when he saw the boy dying whom he had come to love. And to hear this widow's agonizing questions and to see her emotional pain only intensified his grief. Again, we must remind ourselves that Elijah was "a man just like us." The fact that he was a prophet of God did not exempt him from all the human emotions that accompany events such as these. There she stood, holding her dead son in her arms, agony written on her tear-stained face, asking that difficult question—"Why?"

As I reflected on this story, my mind went back many years to an event in my own life. I was only four years old when my sister, Jo Ann, who was just a year younger than I, hurt herself on the edge of a low table in my aunt's living room. We had been visiting that evening, and while running around the room as children do, she had caught the edge of the table with her side.

My parents thought nothing of it until several days later when she began to complain of severe pains. Eventually the local doctor put her in the hospital where they diagnosed her condition as appendicitis. When they opened up her little body they found nothing but a mass of gangrene. In those days there was nothing they could do but sew her back up and hope for a miracle. Just a few days later she died.

I was only four, but I remember the sadness of those days. One event particularly is impressed upon my mind. Several days after the funeral I was playing in the kitchen. My mother was sitting in a chair listening to an old battery-operated radio down on the farm where we lived in Indiana. She was wiping tears from her eyes. I distinctly remember reaching out and tugging her hand, trying to get her to do something. What, I can't remember. But I do remember that she pushed me away and I remember the rejection I felt at that moment. But more so, I remember her instant response when she saw the emotional pain in my own face. Reaching out, she pulled me close and apologized. I remember the words clearly as she said with a tearful voice, "I'm sorry, Gene. I didn't mean to hurt your feelings." And then she explained what she had been listening to over the radio and how it related to Jo Ann's death. And one reason I remember her explanation so clearly was that there before her on the table was a pair of little white shoes—Jo Ann's little shoes. And then she explained to me the song she had been listening to on the radio. The lyrics told the story of a little child who was dying, and she was telling her mother "to put her little shoes away."

I remember so clearly the tears that day, the words of the song, and somehow in my four-year-old heart I understood and I felt deep compassion for my mother. I distinctly remember trying to comfort her.

Death of a loved one brings sadness and heartache. It's very real! There standing before Elijah was a woman with a broken heart. In her arms was a little boy who was no longer breathing. And even more painful to Elijah were the questions she was asking. In her emotional pain she was actually rejecting the man who had saved her life—accusing him of making her aware of her own sin and then taking the life of her son to punish her.

But there was another factor involved in Elijah's emotional response. He had come to this family in the name of God. He had shared his mission and how God had cared for him in the ravine of Kerith. The woman and her son had responded to his message and to his God. They had put their trust in Elijah and in the Lord. And now, her son had died and Elijah was feeling deeply her distrust of both him and the God he represented. There was no human explanation. God's very name and reputation were at stake. What would people say once they found out what happened? Elijah, too, was confused, distraught and fearful!

ELIJAH'S PRAYER
1 Kings 17:19-21

"Give me your son," Elijah replied, no doubt with intense emotion. He then took the boy in his arms, climbed to the upper room where he had been staying, laid him on his own bed and began to pray earnestly for the boy. In fact, we read that "he *cried out* to the Lord." Elijah's own emotional distress and frustration are obvious. "O Lord my God," he cried, "have you brought tragedy also upon this widow I am staying with, by causing her son to die?" (1 Kings 17:19-20).

Elijah then "stretched himself out on the boy three times and cried out to the Lord, 'O Lord my God, let this boy's life return to him' " (17:21). Like Elisha, the man who was to eventually succeed him as a prophet of God in Israel, Elijah probably "lay upon the boy, mouth to mouth, eyes to eyes, hands to hands" (2 Kings 4:34) as he cried to God for mercy.

GOD'S RESPONSE
1 Kings 17:22-24

As so often happens when God's people pray in earnest, the Lord heard and answered Elijah's prayer. Life returned to the boy and "he lived." You can imagine the joy that gripped Elijah's soul as he descended the stairs with the boy in his arms and presented him to his mother. "Look," he said, "your son is alive!" (1 Kings 17:23).

The woman's response must have been just as rewarding to Elijah. "Now I know," she said, "that you are a man of God and that the word of the Lord from your mouth is the truth" (17:24). In these words we discover even more of what had happened as the boy lay dying. As his condition worsened, the widow began to point an accusing finger at Elijah. In reality, she had begun to doubt if Elijah was indeed God's representative. As long as things were going well because of his presence with her, she responded to his message of truth. But when things began to sour, she began to doubt and to point a finger of accusation.

This was a very painful experience for Elijah. Those of us in the ministry, particularly, can identify at least a little with this experience. Almost every pastor can relate experiences when those they've tried to help the most eventually turn on them when things do not go well. To be accused by those you have tried to help of being insincere, uncaring, and lacking of love is very painful.

Elijah, at this moment, also experienced that kind of pain. And we see that pain expressed in his prayer for the boy. He too did not understand what was happening. *Was* he the cause of the boy's death? Had the Lord brought tragedy into this family because of his presence in the home?

At this point in Elijah's life, he too began to question God's ways. It was confusing enough to not understand what was happening, but to be rejected in the process by the one he had saved from starvation was indeed frustrating.

But God honored Elijah's persistence and prayer. In the process, God also honored his honesty and forthrightness regarding his doubts, his fears, and his disillusionment, and his disappointment. He gave the boy new life. And in doing so, the widow's faith was restored and Elijah experienced the joy of seeing his new friends reunited and responding positively to the will of God.

But more important to Elijah and his relationships with this little family was the fact that she no longer rejected the God he served. The Lord's reputation was once again preserved. To Elijah, this was particularly important since his own people had turned to false gods. In essence, this concern was why Elijah was there in the first place—because he had taken this stand for the one true God. It is not surprising that he wanted God's name vindicated and honored.

WHAT CAN WE LEARN FROM THIS OLD TESTAMENT EXPERIENCE?

The most important lesson revolves around Elijah and what God was doing to continue to prepare him for even greater struggles against the forces of evil. All along God had been getting Elijah ready for an encounter, first, with King Ahab and then the prophets of Baal. What Elijah asked God to do for the widow's son would seem minor compared with what he was eventually going to ask God to do on Mount Carmel. The Lord was continuing to prepare Elijah for the task ahead!

The point for us to understand and remember is that *God is preparing us for the big challenges in life when we face the smaller challenges victoriously.*

But the most important lesson we can learn in the process is, *God wants us to understand our motives and why we are asking Him for help.*

Let's look at some of the more specific points the Lord wants to call to our attention.

First, it is in the midst of situations that are beyond our control that we really learn to pray. How true in Elijah's experience! How true in our own!

In some respects it is unfortunate that we have to be in a position where our backs are against the wall before we take the privilege of prayer seriously. But this has always been true in the history of God's people. And God understands our human tendencies. In these situations He does not turn a deaf ear. Though the outcome is not always what we might choose, He responds with what is best.

So we should not hesitate to pray when we are facing serious problems, even though we've been neglecting this important spiritual exercise. It is only natural that we pray more during this kind of trial and that we pray more intently.

Second, God understands our anxieties, our fears, our disappointments and our disillusionments. We should not be fearful of expressing these thoughts and feelings to Him in prayer.

Some people see God as an angry father figure who is ready to punish when they share how they really feel. Not so! If that were true, God would act before we speak, for He clearly knows what we think and feel. Consequently, we might as well tell Him.

But we must also remember that He is God. He cannot be manipulated. But there are times that He responds in unusual ways, especially when His reputation and name are at stake.

This is illustrated in a very unique way when Moses was on Mount Sinai receiving the laws of God. While there, Israel built the golden calf and bowed down to it. They even had the audacity to give credit to this idol for bringing them out of Egypt.

Predictably, the Lord was angry at the children of Israel, so much so He told Moses to step aside so that He might destroy them. But Moses reminded God that if he wiped Israel "off the face of the earth," the Egyptians would say, "It was with evil intent that [you] brought them out, to kill them in the mountains" (Exod. 32:12). In other words, God's reputation and name were at stake.

We cannot explain satisfactorily how a man could change God's mind by reminding Him of His reputation, but it's true! We read that "the Lord relented and did not bring on his people the disaster he had threatened" (32:14).

Third, God is particularly responsive to our prayers when we are able to get beyond our own interests and concerns and focus on other people's needs, but especially on His reputation. Though he felt personal rejection, Elijah's prayers were based on his concern for the widow and, most of all, he was concerned about God's reputation. After all, he was identified as a "man of *God*"—a man who represented the one true God. For tragedy to strike in this instance would cause unbelievers to question even more the message Elijah was proclaiming. How obvious this was from the widow's response!

When we pray for God's help are we concerned about ourselves rather than how these events we're experiencing affect others and the Lord's reputation? If we focused more on the needs of others and the name of the God we serve, would we not experience more answers to prayer? I think so!

Don't misunderstand. He wants us to share our needs. Paul, writing to the Philippians, said, "Do not be anxious about *anything,* but in *everything,* by prayer and petition, with thanksgiving, present your requests to God" (Phil. 4:6). God is concerned about our needs—whatever they are.

But even so, God's reputation should be first—not ours! His will should be first—not ours!! His name should be first—not ours!

I remember a personal experience when I had come to that point in my own life. I was deeply distressed and burdened and spent a great deal of time in prayer about the matter. But one day, when there wasn't anything more that I could do to try to solve the problem, I finally came to the place where I realized that I was really more concerned about Gene's reputation than God's. In retrospect, I now understand that I did not see that reality until there was nothing more that Gene could do! And when I was finally able to cry out to the Lord with that kind of honesty and openness, God heard my prayers. I remember that moment when I said to the Lord, "Lord, it's your reputation that's important, not mine." And from that moment, the clouds of despair began to roll away and the sun began to shine.

This does not mean that we should not pray for ourselves—and our own needs and concerns. But it does mean that we ought to ask ourselves *why* we're praying for ourselves. There's an ultimate concern that should guide even this kind of praying—God's name, God's honor, God's integrity—and His will!

And remember too that God can bring honor to Himself in all situations, no matter what the outcome. In this instance, God answered Elijah's prayer and restored the boy because it would bring the most honor to his name. But there are times when He can bring more honor to His name in the midst of human tragedy.

ONE FINAL QUESTION

How do we respond if God does not answer our specific prayers for physical healing?

First, we must realize that God has never promised to heal all physical infirmities, even though we pray in faith. He *has* promised, however, to provide grace and strength for every situation, but not always to provide deliverance from death.

As we've already observed in chapter 2, the Apostle Paul illustrates this in his own life. Though Paul often healed people with God's power, there came a time in his life when God did not answer his own prayers for personal healing. Writing to the Corinthians, he informed them he had asked the Lord three times to heal him. In fact, he said, "I pleaded with the Lord to take it away from me." However, the Lord's response to Paul was that His grace was sufficient for him (2 Cor. 12:8-9).

It is important to understand this point, for an inaccurate

view of God's sovereignty in healing can lead people to false guilt, feeling they are to blame for illness that is not cured through prayer. Remember that God's will is more important than ours in these matters, and when it comes to physical healing He has chosen not to reveal His particular will.

On the other hand, God does choose to respond to our prayers for healing when it is His will. Furthermore, if we do not pray, He may not respond. Prayer, then, does make a difference, whether He responds with healing or with grace to enable us to bear the burden.

5

Facing Pressures in the World

Following Elijah's traumatic experience in praying for the widow's son and the subsequent experience of joy in seeing God answer his prayer and restore the boy to life, there came another time of waiting for the predetermined period of drought to run its course. How long, we're not sure, but it could have been another two years. James tells us specifically that "it did not rain on the land for three and a half years" (Jas. 5:17). It probably took six months for Ahab to take the drought seriously, at which time Elijah went into hiding. Assuming he spent approximately a year in the ravine at Kerith, Elijah would have approximately another two years from the beginning of his stay with the widow of Sidon. Nevertheless, we read, "After a *long time*, in the *third year*, the word of the Lord came to Elijah: 'Go and present yourself to Ahab, and I will send rain on the land' " (1 Kings 18:1).[1]

All of these events were preparing Elijah for what was to be his greatest spiritual battle of all—a direct confrontation with the forces of evil as they revealed themselves through the prophets of Baal. But since Elijah was "a man just like us," his preparation for this gigantic task also involved a need for rest and relaxation. Following his difficult battle against death, it seems God gave him an extended period of time to rehabilitate—to rest, relax, and reflect on God's providential care, His tremendous power, and His righteousness and holiness. Elijah was getting ready for a dramatic and stressful encounter, first with Ahab, then with the children of Israel and the prophets of Baal, and finally with Jezebel herself. And when God once again spoke to him directly, Elijah was ready. There was no debate, no ifs and buts, no hesitancy. We simply read, "So Elijah went to present himself to Ahab" (18:2).

But before he reached Ahab, he had another brief encounter—a face-to-face meeting with an old friend—a man named Obadiah. Though brief and rather uneventful for Elijah, it was destined to be very traumatic for Obadiah.

OBADIAH'S STRATEGIC POSITION
1 Kings 18:3

Who was this man Obadiah? The historical record tells us two very important facts. *First,* he "was in charge" of Ahab's palace; *second,* he "was a devout believer in the Lord" (1 Kings 18:3). From a human perspective this was an unbelievable combination. From God's point of view He has always had people in strategic positions to accomplish His will. There was Joseph who became prime minister of Egypt, a strategic position that not only saved the people of Egypt from the destructive force of a severe famine, but also provided the context for God to raise up the nation He had promised He would—the nation of Israel. Later, Moses eventually found himself as heir to the throne of Egypt, and after forty years in the wilderness, came back to Egypt to lead Israel out of captivity. Daniel also emerged as one of the most influential men in the Babylonian and Medo-Per-

sian empires. And Nehemiah served as cupbearer to King
Artaxerxes. And we must not forget Esther, who because of
her strategic position saved her people from unusual difficulties and problems.

In each of these situations God enabled His people to
occupy key positions in the secular, pagan world in order to
accomplish His divine purposes. Most often, that position
set the stage for God to accomplish His divine purposes
through His chosen people—Israel.

Obadiah too occupied such a position. He was in charge
of Ahab's palace. He was the king's trusted administrator
and confidant. With this position went open-ended responsibility and authority. And though Ahab was king of Israel,
he was in many respects "pagan" in both his personal life-
style and in his approach to leadership.

At the same time, Obadiah was a "believer in the Lord."
But he was more! He "was a *devout* believer." He had not
compromised his faith in the living God. Unlike the king he
served, he did not worship the prophets of Baal.

Think about this for a moment! How could this be? How
was it possible to be in this strategic position, serving a king
who was promoting the worst kind of pagan idolatry, and
yet be a devout believer? How was it possible to be this
kind of person and yet maintain Ahab's trust? How was it
possible to keep from being suspect? But there's more!

OBADIAH'S INCREDIBLE PLAN
1 Kings 18:4

These questions become even more mind-boggling
when we discover Obadiah's undercover operations.
"While Jezebel was killing off the Lord's prophets," Obadiah was protecting them. He "had taken a hundred" of
these men and had "hidden them in two caves, fifty in
each." And furthermore, he had "supplied them with food
and water" (1 Kings 18:4).

At this point we can draw several conclusions. *First,*

Obadiah was a devout believer—very devout! His spiritual convictions were "fleshed out" in a way that is hard to comprehend. His life hung in the balance every second of every twenty-four-hour day. Had someone in Ahab's palace other than Obadiah's own trusted servants become suspicious, it would have meant certain death. Even at that, he had no guarantee that one of his own servants would not let the word slip out. This was no cat-and-mouse game. This was a battle against Satan and his evil forces. And no one knew the danger more intensely than Obadiah. His choice was deliberate, knowing full well he could be executed at any moment.

What would cause a man to put both his strategic position and his life in jeopardy? The Scriptures tell us. He "was a *devout* believer in the Lord." God was central in all he did. Obeying the Lord was more important to Obadiah than anything else in life—including life itself.

But there is a *second* thing we can conclude from Obadiah's "strategic position" and his "incredible plan." He was not only a committed and courageous believer, but *he was a very wise man*. It was, of course, his wisdom that enabled him to eventually fill such a strategic position in the king's palace. But it would take wisdom *beyond* human ingenuity to both develop and implement such an incredible plan to save the Lord's prophets. How Obadiah did it, no one really knows. Someday in heaven it will be exciting to ask him. To be sure, we can speculate that whatever he says, it will be prefaced with one profound exclamation! "Without God, I could have done nothing."

OBADIAH'S PREDICTABLE PREDICAMENT
1 Kings 18:5-16

It's only logical to conclude that Obadiah encountered gigantic problems in carrying out his plan. In fact, he probably faced them daily. But he did not anticipate what would happen when suddenly he encountered Elijah.

As the effects of the drought began to press in harder and harder, Ahab ordered Obadiah to assist him in finding food for his horses and mules so they wouldn't have to kill them. Ironically, he was more concerned that his animals live than the Lord's prophets. The king went in one direction and Obadiah in another, searching for springs and valleys where grass might still be growing (1 Kings 18:4-6).

"As Obadiah was walking along," Elijah met him, coming from the opposite direction. Although Obadiah recognized this man of God who had disappeared from sight some three years before, he needed reassurance. "Is it really you, my lord Elijah?" he asked (18:7).

Elijah's answer, of course, was affirmative and reassuring. But his larger response was shocking and threatening to Obadiah. "Go tell your master, 'Elijah is here,' " he added (18:8).

Obadiah was immediately defensive. The tension he had lived with for nearly three years was obvious. "What have I done wrong," he asked, "that you are handing your servant over to Ahab to be put to death?" (18:9).

At this juncture Obadiah filled in the historical outline alluded to in the previous verses. Ahab, influence by his wicked queen, had sent "secret service" men to every conceivable place to look for Elijah. And wherever the report was negative from those interrogated, Ahab had demanded a sworn confession that they had not seen Elijah nor did they know where he was.

Obadiah knew it might mean certain death for him to report back to Ahab that he had encountered Elijah but had not brought him in. Furthermore, even if Obadiah survived such an ordeal, he was terribly frightened that Elijah might not be there when Ahab returned to find him. "I don't know where the Spirit of the Lord may carry you when I leave you," he said. "If I go and tell Ahab and he doesn't find you, he will kill me" (18:12).

Obadiah's intense fear and frustration are even more

obvious in his next statements. He reminded Elijah of his faithfulness to God—serving and worshiping the Lord since his youth. With deep emotion he reviewed how he had jeopardized his own life daily by hiding the Lord's prophets in caves and providing them with food and water. "And *now*," he pleaded, "*now* you tell me to go to my master and say 'Elijah is here.' He will kill me!" (18:14).

Elijah understood and sympathized with Obadiah's predicament. He assured him that he would *not* disappear off the scene. "As the Lord Almighty lives, whom I serve," he said, "I will surely present myself to Ahab today" (18:15).

What actually transpired further between this courageous prophet and his faithful friend Obadiah, we can only speculate. Elijah no doubt briefed him on all that had happened while he was in hiding—how God had cared for him and protected him. He also must have convinced Obadiah it was now *God's time* for him to encounter Ahab face to face. Indeed, it was the Lord who had said to Elijah, "Go and present yourself to Ahab, and I will send rain on the land" (18:1).

To what extent Obadiah's fears were dissipated, we don't know. After all, he had lived consistently with fear in Ahab's court. Nevertheless, we know that he was reassured. He responded to Elijah's order. He returned to Ahab's palace and told the king Elijah was waiting to meet him. Predictably Ahab went immediately to meet Elijah. But that's another story! At this point in our study we need to ask and answer a very important question.

WHAT CAN A TWENTIETH-CENTURY CHRISTIAN LIKE ME LEARN FROM A MAN LIKE OBADIAH?

First, God wants to use Christians who are in key positions in a secular and pagan society to accomplish His purpose in the world. What is God's primary purpose for the Christian in this world? Certainly God is desirous of protecting His children. But there is a purpose in God's mind that is far more basic than our protection and sense of security in this life. He is interested in communicating His message of redemption to a lost world. Christians are to be *salt* and *light*. Jesus said, "You are the *salt* of the earth . . . . You are the *light* of the world" (Matt. 5:13-14). And as we fulfill God's desire as dynamic witnesses in the world, we are building the kingdom of God—not a kingdom on this earth. God's primary purpose for Christians is not to preserve our society. Neither is His primary purpose to provide a place of security for His children. These are all worthy objectives, but they should not be ends in themselves.

This was Paul's message to Timothy. We are to pray "for kings and all those in authority, that we may live peaceful and quiet lives in all godliness and holiness" (1 Tim. 2:2). Thus God *is* interested in our sense of security. But that purpose is secondary. The reason we are to pray for government leaders is that they might provide an environment where it is possible to share the good news of Jesus Christ. Thus Paul culminates this injunction, "This is good, and pleases God our Savior, who wants *all men to be saved* and to come to a knowledge of the truth" (2:3-4). There is one basic message that they desperately need: "For there is one God and one mediator between God and men, the man Christ Jesus, who gave himself as a ransom for all men" (1 Tim. 2:5-6).

Every Christian who rubs shoulders with a non-Christian is in a strategic position. Our greatest influence can be felt, not through statements about morality, but through flesh-and-blood contacts with people, reflecting our faith in God, our eternal hope for the future and our love for God and one another. As the world is deteriorating, leaving people reaping the results of their own moral choices, they are searching frantically for something to give meaning to life.

Every Christian has the answer to their dilemma. It is a personal relationship with Jesus Christ that gives hope for the present and the future. Furthermore, it is loving, moral, and ethical relationships with other Christians who provide encouragement and flesh out that hope and security while we occupy our position on planet earth.

Second, God can only use Christians effectively to accomplish His purpose in the world who are truly devoted to Him. Obadiah illustrates this fact beautifully. He had served the Lord from his youth. And every biblical character who has occupied a strategic position in a secular situation and has been used by God in unusual ways emerged as this kind of person. So must every twentieth-century Christian!

We will never impress the world by being like them. Our value system must reflect God's standard of righteousness and holiness. Peter said it well. "Dear friends," he wrote, "I urge you, as aliens and strangers in the world, to abstain from sinful desires, which war against your soul. Live such good lives among the pagans that, though they accuse you of doing wrong, they may see your good deeds and glorify God on the day he visits us" (1 Pet. 2:11-12).

Peter is telling us in this passage that it is possible to live for Christ and reflect His holiness in most instances without alienating non-Christians. They may not agree with us, but down deep they will respect us. They may laugh at us publicly but admire us privately. Most non-Christians respect people who are willing to take a moral and ethical stand.

Many Christians alienate non-Christians unnecessarily. In most instances it is not their convictions, but how they communicate their convictions. And this leads us to our next lesson from Obadiah.

Third, God uses Christians in a special way who reflect wisdom in their relationships with non-Christians. Jesus, sending His disciples out into a very hostile world that has probably not been equalled since, said, "I am sending you out like sheep among wolves. Therefore be as shrewd as snakes and as innocent as doves" (Matt. 10:16).

Today there are many Christians who are not acting wisely in their efforts to counteract the current evil trends in our society. Their strategy is bombastic and offensive. Their behavior is defiant and aggressive. Many are responding out of threat and fear rather than out of deep concern for others. They are often more emotional than rational. In the process, they are violating biblical principles, causing non-Christians to respond in anger.

Furthermore, the message of Christ and salvation is lost in the battle. Rather than being salt and light, many believers are causing non-Christians to "spew them out of their mouths." They are devout, but devout in the wrong way. Their "devotedness" is reflected in aggressive attitudes and actions towards non-Christians rather than in their relationship with God.

For example, Christian leaders have been imprisoned in the United States because they have refused to meet government requirements for conducting Christian schools. They have openly defied the laws of our society that are designed to protect our children from unnecessary harm. Their actions are a direct violation of Peter's exhortation, "Submit yourselves for the Lord's sake to every authority instituted among men" (1 Pet. 2:13).

Obviously there are times when a Christian should refuse to cooperate with the government. For example, many Christians in the early centuries chose to die when they were asked to deny that Jesus Christ was their Lord and Master. But even this kind of action was not to be done with a defiant attitude. Many of these Christians went to their death submissively and without anger towards those who caused it all. Like Jesus Christ, they said, "Father, forgive them, for they do not know what they are doing" (Luke 23:34).

There is also talk among some Christians, advocating that it would be perfectly legitimate to refuse to pay taxes because of sinful actions on the part of government leaders. The rationale is that we should refuse to allow our money to be used to fund immoral behavior. This is an interesting philosophy in view of the fact that Jesus told His disciples to "give to Caesar what is Caesar's, and to God what is God's" (Matt. 22:21). This is a significant exhortation in view of the fact that the Roman government was guilty of many insidious and heinous crimes.

Many Christians today are reacting in unwise ways to changes in our culture. And it's understandable why people are nervous. Our social values are changing. More so, it's impacting our children. But we must not resist in unwise ways. To do so is a violation of both the commands and the principles of Scripture. Furthermore, it often makes our witness in the world ineffective.

Fourth, to be God's person in a secular society often leads to predicaments, but God delights in using these problems to achieve His purposes. Where there are no problems there is no need for solutions. Where there are no battles there are no victories. It is in the context of tension that God most often reveals His power and His love. Furthermore, it is in the midst of persecution that a Christian can truly reveal his commitment and love for Jesus Christ. It is in the midst of temptation that Christians can demonstrate commitment to Jesus Christ and bear witness of His power to deliver from temptation and sin.

Paul wrote, "Everyone who wants to live a godly life in Christ Jesus will be persecuted." He stated further that "evil men and impostors will go from bad to worse, deceiving and being deceived" (2 Tim. 3:12-13). In view of this prophecy, it should not surprise us that our environment is changing for the worse! God said it would.

It should not alarm us, then, when we find ourselves in predicaments because of our position in a secular society. These are God's opportunities to demonstrate His divine message through our lives. He has a unique way of being able to turn lemons into lemonade and stumbling blocks into stepping stones if we'll let Him.

True, there will be times when we're fearful and frustrated. So was Obadiah. There'll be times when we need reassurance and encouragement. So did Obadiah. There'll be times when we conclude there is no solution to the problem. So did Obadiah. But there *was* a solution. God's purpose was fulfilled. This we'll see in future chapters.

PERSONAL RESPONSE

1. To what extent am I allowing God to use me to accomplish His purpose in this world—
- on the job
- in my neighborhood
- at school
- in my recreational and social activities?

2. To what extent am I living a devoted life for Jesus Christ, and at the same time being wise and tactful in my relationships with non-Christians?

3. To what extent do I view predicaments as God's opportunities to demonstrate His power and love through my life?

ACTION STEP

Think of one opportunity you have to be an effective witness for Christ. Ask God to help you turn that opportunity into a fruitful experience.

Note

1. Since God's command for Elijah to go and see Ahab happened in the third year, and the encounter with the prophets of Baal was near at hand, after which it rained again, some commentators believe that the historical record in 1 Kings is calculated from the time Elijah went into hiding. In other words, the period before he fled to the ravine of Kerith is estimated to be about six months. There would then be another three years of drought, and God's command to go and see King Ahab would come in the third year, but probably at the end of that year. This calculation would then correspond to James's statement that the drought lasted for three and one half years (Jas. 5:17).

6

The Dangers of
Rationalization

You can imagine Ahab's surprise when Obadiah returned from his journey and reported that he had met Elijah. For more than three years Ahab had been combing the country for the man who was responsible for the drought that plagued Israel. Furthermore, you can imagine Ahab's consternation when Obadiah informed him that Elijah was waiting to see him. Whatever his emotional reactions, he wasted no time in getting there.

AHAB'S RATIONALIZATION
1 Kings 18:16-17

As soon as Ahab saw Elijah, he asked a very revealing question. "Is that you, you troubler of Israel?" (1 Kings 18:17), he must have asked with a snarling voice. Inherent in this question is a deep-rooted problem that has affected all humanity, a social disease that has infected every man and woman who has ever lived on planet Earth. Ever since sin entered the human race, our tendency has been to shift the blame for our own irresponsible behavior to someone else. This we call rationalization.

Adam and Eve (Gen. 3:1-13)

Interestingly, Adam was the first man to rationalize his wrongdoing when God confronted him in the garden after he and Eve had disobeyed. When the Lord asked him if he had eaten from the tree they were to avoid, Adam responded, "The *woman* you put here with me—she gave me some fruit from the tree, and I ate it" (Gen. 3:12). In actuality, Adam was not only shifting the blame to Eve, but to God. Though he was referring to Eve, he made it clear that *God* gave her to him.

Eve was the second person to rationalize. When the Lord asked her what she had done, she replied, "The *serpent* deceived me, and I ate" (3:13). In other words, she was saying, "The devil made me do it." She shifted the blame to Satan.

What was the primary reason that caused both Adam and Eve to rationalize? Adam himself made it clear when he said, "I was afraid" (3:10). *Fear* is often at the root of rationalization.

It should not surprise us, then, that all of us have difficulty facing up to the negative consequences of our personal attitudes and actions. It is a direct result of the spiritual disease the Bible identifies as sin. And one of the primary manifestations of sin is fear—fear of rejection, fear of punishment, fear of facing the consequences of our own actions.

Abraham and Sarah (Gen. 16:1-5)

Time and again the problem of rationalization crops up in human relationships. When Sarah was unable to bear children she convinced her husband Abraham to have a child by her maidservant, Hagar. This seems strange and immoral to us—and it is—but it was a common practice in the pagan world of Abraham's day. In fact, many marriage contracts actually included a clause indicating that if a wife could not bear children she would be responsible to provide a substitute woman who could, so the family name could be carried on.

Abraham cooperated with Sarah's plan and Hagar bore him a son. But things did not turn out as Sarah had hoped. When Hagar became pregnant, "she began to despise her mistress" (Gen. 16:4). Like her first parents, Sarah would not acknowledge her mistake and take the blame. "*You* are responsible for the wrong I am suffering," she said to her husband. "I put my servant in your arms, and now that she knows she is pregnant, she despises me" (16:5).

Sarah introduces us to another primary reason we rationalize—jealousy and its accompanying emotion, anger. How quickly this combination of feelings can take over in our lives and cause us to blame others for our own actions.

Moses and Aaron (Exod. 32:1-23)

When Moses ascended Mount Sinai to receive the tablets of stone on which God wrote the Ten Commandments, the children of Israel grew restless. They approached Moses' brother Aaron and said, "Come, make us gods who will go before us. As for this fellow Moses who brought us up out of Egypt, we don't know what has happened to him" (Exod. 32:1).

Aaron responded, molded a golden calf, and built an altar. The people bowed down to the false god and offered sacrifices and committed immoralities as part of their pagan worship.

When Moses returned with God's laws, after convincing the Lord to spare Israel from severe judgment because of their flagrant idolatry, he confronted his brother with what he had done. Aaron's response is again reflective of the process of rationalization. "Do not be angry, my lord,"

Aaron answered. "You know how prone *these people* are to evil. They said to me, 'Make us gods who will go before us. As for this fellow Moses who brought us up out of Egypt, we don't know what has happened to him.' So I told them, 'Whoever has any gold jewelry, take it off.' Then they gave me the gold, and I threw it into the fire, and *out came this calf!*" (32:22-24).

Rather than admitting that he, Aaron, had sinned, he shifted the blame to his fellow Israelites. Furthermore, he came up with the incredible explanation that the calf somehow emerged from the fire without his help. This is indeed interesting in view of the fact that the sacred record specifically states that "He took what they handed him and made it into an idol cast in the shape of a calf, *fashioning it with a tool*" (32:4). No wonder Jeremiah wrote, "The heart is deceitful above all things and beyond cure. Who can understand it?" (Jer. 17:9).

What caused Aaron to rationalize? It certainly involved all of the emotions outlined thus far. But there is more. His initial behavior was no doubt motivated by a need for *prestige* and *power*. Operating in Moses' shadow to this point, he now had an opportunity to lead Israel. And when confronted with his sin, these needs, blended with fear of rejection, caused him to explain what had happened with a dishonest, self-protecting response.

Saul and Samuel (1 Sam. 15:1-23)

When Saul was anointed king, the Lord instructed him to attack the Amalekites and to destroy them because of what they had done to Israel in mercilessly attacking them in the wilderness. He was to spare nothing including "cattle and sheep, camels and donkeys" (1 Sam. 15:3).

But Saul disobeyed. He kept "the best of . . . everything that was good" (15:9). The Lord was deeply grieved and so was Samuel. Samuel went to see Saul and confronted him with his disobedience. Again we see rationalization at work in Saul's response. He answered, "The *soldiers* brought them from the Amalekites. *They* spared the best of the sheep and cattle to sacrifice to the Lord your God" (15:15).

With this response Saul was shifting the blame to his men. However, the biblical text clearly states that "*Saul* and the army spared . . . everything that was good" (15:9).

We get an additional insight into the process of rationalization from Saul's experience. Following his disobedience, Saul went to Carmel and "set up a monument *in his own honor*" (15:12). Pride is also an important factor in rationalization. It certainly helps explain why Adam blamed Eve, why Eve blamed Satan, why Sarah blamed Abraham, and why Aaron blamed the people. And it certainly helps explain why Saul blamed his army.

Pilate and Jesus (Matt. 27:1-24)

The most dramatic illustration of rationalization is recorded in the New Testament. It involved Pilate, who was responsible under Roman law to make a decision regarding Jesus Christ. Though he found no fault in the Lord, he "handed him over to be crucified" (Matt. 27:26). But before doing so, "he took water and washed his hands in front of the crowd . . . 'I am innocent of this man's blood,' he said. 'It is *your* responsibility' " (27:24).

Pilate turned an innocent Man over to be put to death, but in his own mind convinced himself he was not to blame. And with this irresponsible act he was trying to relieve his own conscience of the guilt he felt—another factor causing rationalization.

And so it was with King Ahab. Though he had caused the trouble that had come on Israel because of his idolatry, he shifted the blame to Elijah. "Is that you, you troubler of Israel?" he asked! (1 Kings 18:17).

Ahab and Naboth (1 Kings 21:1-29)

What caused Ahab's rationalization? No doubt it was a combination of factors as it always is. But as with the other biblical characters who were guilty of this self-deceptive and defensive behavior, there seem to be some unique factors in Ahab's personality.

This is clearly illustrated in an experience Ahab had with a man by the name of Naboth. This man owned a vineyard that was located near Ahab's palace. When the king noticed the vineyard, he wanted it for a vegetable garden. He offered to buy the vineyard or to replace it with another in a different location.

The vineyard was special to Naboth because he had received it as an inheritance. He rejected the king's offer, which made Ahab "sullen and angry" (1 Kings 21:4). Ahab went home, threw himself across his bed and lay there, "sulking and refused to eat" (21:4). When Jezebel, his wife, found out, she asked, "Why are you so sullen? Why won't you eat?" (21:5).

After Ahab explained what had happened, Jezebel took matters into her own hands. As only she could do, she devised a scheme to have Naboth accused of blasphemy against both God and the king. Consequently he was killed. When Ahab "heard that Naboth was dead, he got up and went down to take possession of Naboth's vineyard" (21:16).

What a sad commentary on Ahab's personality! He was incredibly selfish and horribly spoiled. Furthermore, he was a weak, passive little man who acted more like a child than an adult.

Think of it! Here was the king of Israel, who was wealthier than any other man in the nation, sulking because he couldn't have a poor man's vineyard to turn into a vegetable garden.

Ahab, then, blamed Elijah for his troubles because he was a weak, self-centered man who fell victim to an evil, dominating, and manipulating wife who used him to achieve her own selfish goals.

ELIJAH'S CONFRONTATION
1 Kings 18:18-19

Elijah dealt with Ahab's rationalization head-on. "I have not made trouble for Israel," Elijah replied. "But you and your father's family have. You have abandoned the Lord's commands and have followed the Baals." (1 Kings 18:18).

Elijah further challenged Ahab to a contest on Mount Carmel. "Now summon the people from all over Israel to meet me on Mount Carmel," he said. "And bring the four hundred and fifty prophets of Baal and the four hundred prophets of Asherah, who eat at Jezebel's table" (18:19).

There's only one way to deal with rationalization. Elijah illustrates how. It must be confronted. Truth must prevail. Self-deception must be unveiled.

Unfortunately, Ahab would not listen. He was too proud and arrogant and had convinced himself that he could do battle with the God of Abraham, Isaac, and Jacob. And because of his refusal to listen, he was headed for a terrible downfall and eventual death. Unfortunately, in the process he would take a number of people down with him.

David and Bathsheba (2 Sam. 12:1-23)

On the positive side, the Scriptures record the story of a man who *did* listen when he was confronted about his sin after he had rationalized it away. He also was a king of Israel. He was not guilty of *idolatry*. Rather, it was *adultery* and, eventually, murder. His name was David. He stole another man's wife, got her pregnant, and then had her husband killed in battle in order to try to cover his own sin.

The Lord sent Nathan to confront David. Nathan's approach, however, was far more subtle but in some respects more potent than Elijah's. He told David a story about a rich man who "had a very large number of sheep and cattle." By contrast there was a poor man who "had nothing except a little ewe lamb he had bought." Nathan went on to explain that the little lamb was very special to this man. "He raised it, and it grew up with him and his children. It shared his food, drank from his cup and even slept in his arms. It was like a daughter to him" (2 Sam. 12:2-3).

One day a man was traveling through and stopped at the rich man's home for a meal. Rather than "taking one of his own sheep or cattle to prepare a meal for the traveler . . . he took the ewe lamb that belonged to the poor man and prepared it for the one who had come to him" (12:4).

David's response was one of intense anger. Being a shepherd most of his early life he could emotionally identify with the situation. How often he must have held a little ewe lamb in his arms, perhaps even feeding it from his own cup and sleeping at night holding it in his arms. David had been a sensitive shepherd.

"As surely as the Lord lives, the man who did this deserves to die!" David responded (12:5).

David was totally caught off guard by Nathan's response. "You are the man!" he said. He went on to explain how he, the king of Israel, had been guilty of an even greater crime. He had taken away Bathsheba, Uriah's *only* wife, while he had *many*. And at that point Nathan pronounced judgment on David for his sin.

David's response was far different from Ahab's. "I have sinned against the Lord," he cried (12:13). At this point his rationalization, motivated by lust and fear, turned to honesty. He faced the reality of what he had done. He made no excuses but threw himself upon God's mercy. And because his heart was softened before the Lord and he repented, God had mercy upon David. Though he paid desperately for his sin in the lives of his own children, he turned back to God.

RATIONALIZATION AND TODAY'S CHRISTIAN

Because of our human weaknesses and sinful natures, all of us as human beings are vulnerable to rationalization. Like those people illustrated in Scripture, there may be various reasons why we rationalize and blame other people for our irresponsible behavior.

Is it fear? Ever since Adam and Eve rationalized because of fear, so have people everywhere. Husbands blame wives and wives blame husbands. Parents blame children and children blame parents. We blame one another and God for our irresponsible behavior.

The Bible states that "perfect love casts out fear." We need not be afraid of God, because this perfect love is available to all mankind. His wrath fell on His Son, Jesus Christ, who bore the sins of the whole world. Rather than blaming others for our human weakness we should face reality, confess our sins, and accept forgiveness in Christ.

NOTE: Children often rationalize out of fear because of adults who are too insensitive and severe in their discipline. In this sense, God holds parents responsible. However, a child may grow up to live an irresponsible life because of our foolish mistakes. At that point he is responsible. There comes a time when every man must bear his own burdens, no matter what the cause.

Is it jealousy? Jealousy is a withering emotion. It withers our souls and alienates us from others. It also appears early in life. In fact, with the capacity to show affection comes a capacity to be jealous. Its feelings are often twin emotions—one positive and the other negative.

Jealousy is also a very strong emotion. It is often at the root of rationalization. For example, Mary is always criticizing Jane for the way she does things—the way she walks, the way she dresses, the way she relates to others. Furthermore, she doesn't believe Jane likes her.

In actuality, Mary resents Jane's ability to sing. She also resents the fact that Jane is asked to sing more often than she is. Mary is jealous, but won't admit it to herself or others. Therefore, from Mary's point of view, Jane is always the focus of the problem, not her.

Is it anger? All of us do things we regret because of anger. But it is difficult to admit it and oftentimes we blame our irresponsible actions on others or on other reasons.

For example, Bill frequently loses his temper. When he does, he feels bad. But rather than admitting his problem and asking forgiveness, he blames his problems on his ill health. It is amazing how often he "develops" a headache *after* he loses his temper rather than *before*. In other words, he often "becomes" ill after he loses his temper in order to justify his aggressive actions.

The Bible says a Christian should be "quick to listen, slow to speak and slow to become angry, for man's anger does not bring about the righteous life that God desires" (Jas. 1:19-20).

Is it a need for security? Every time Jim is afraid of failure, he conjures up numerous reasons why he should not participate in a particular activity. Either he is too busy, too tired or too something else. Unable to face his real problem, he excuses his actions with more legitimate and socially acceptable reasons.

Is it pride? More people rationalize because of pride than any other reason. And this should not surprise us. It caused Satan's downfall.

Whenever we fail at something, we become ego involved. John is a classic example. A good athlete, he is intensely competitive. But he often plays tennis with men who outclass him. And when he loses, he always makes excuses. Often he is "out of shape," or "didn't get much sleep the night before," or "he had something on his mind." Several of these things may be true, of course, but he will never admit that the other person is just a better tennis player than he is. John's problem is *pride* combined, of course, with a sense of insecurity.

Is it guilt? Guilt is a very elusive emotion and often causes us to engage in activities that are associated with some type of obsessive-compulsive behavior. Pilate "washed his hands" when he turned the innocent Son of God over to a howling mob to be crucified. Today some people do the same thing to cover up their guilt. It may involve bathing, scrubbing, and polishing, or it may involve being excessively neat, tidy, and organized. This behavior involves actions that are often motivated by guilt that has been repressed from consciousness.

Unfortunately, some people engage in this kind of obsessive-compulsive behavior because of *false* guilt. It often begins in childhood because of parents who are too strict. Sometimes it relates to being a part of a legalistic religious system that has developed a standard of conduct that is cultural rather than biblical.

Is it selfishness? Some people blame others for problems because they are self-centered and egocentric. The world revolves around themselves. No matter what happens, the blame belongs on someone else. They never accept their share of responsibility.

Self-centered people take advantage of others and they are never satisfied with what they have. This was certainly true of Ahab.

Is it lust? Physical and psychological appetites cause incredible rationalization. For example, some Christians justify exposing themselves to carnal experiences in order to discover what is "going on in the world." After all, they say, we can't be an effective witness in the world without knowing how the world lives.

To a certain extent this may be true. But therein lies the danger. It makes it easier to rationalize. A true test of our motives is the extent we want *more* and *more* exposure to the world's system. Chances are we are simply justifying our fleshly actions with an acceptable reason not acceptable to ourselves.

All Christians must beware of rationalization! It is often painful to be honest with ourselves. And it is true we can be self-deceived without knowing it. That is why it is so important to listen carefully to the voice of God through the Word of God. Yes, "the heart is deceitful above all things and beyond cure. Who can understand it?" The answer is that the Lord can. He can cure us of our sin. Jeremiah acknowledges that when he says, "I the Lord search the heart and examine the mind" (Jer. 17:9-10).

Furthermore, we read in Scripture that "the word of God is living and active. Sharper than any double-edged sword, it penetrates even to dividing soul and spirit, joints and marrow; it judges the thoughts and attitudes of the heart" (Heb. 4:12). With David we should pray, "Search me, O God, and know my heart; test me and know my anxious thoughts. See if there is any offensive way in me, and lead me in the way everlasting" (Ps. 139:23-24). Be assured, God will answer that prayer!

PERSONAL RESPONSE

1. When was the last time you rationalized your attitudes and actions and blamed someone else for your irresponsible behavior?

2. What caused it?

☐ Fear
☐ Jealousy
☐ Anger
☐ Fear of failure
☐ Pride
☐ Guilt
☐ Selfishness
☐ Lust
☐ Other _____

ACTION STEPS

- Confess your sin to God.
- Accept His forgiveness.
- Acknowledge it to the person or persons you've tried to deceive.
- Decide by God's grace to deal with the cause and to avoid self-deception and rationalization.
- Read the Word of God regularly and ask God to help you to live an honest, upright life.

NOTE: If you are sincerely trying to overcome your problem through confessions, prayer, and obedience to the Word of God and yet cannot experience victory, your problem may be more psychological than spiritual. If so, seek help from a competent Christian counselor who can help you understand and overcome your problem.

Be careful, however! A tendency at this juncture is to rationalize, for it is easier to blame our problem on a "psychological cause," rather than face the fact that we must bear final responsibility for our actions. If our problems are more psychological than spiritual, the roots often go back to our relationships with our parents. How easy it becomes to blame them for our present behavior and go right on behaving irresponsibly. If we do, that indeed is rationalization!

7

Avoiding Double-Mindedness

When God spoke to Elijah at the time he was residing at
the widow's home in Zarephath and said, "Go and present
yourself to Ahab" (1 Kings 18:1), we are only given a brief
sketch of what Elijah was to do. However, from his prayer
on Mount Carmel, we know that the details were clear to
Elijah (18:36). He knew what lay ahead. Though he was
walking by faith, it was faith based on the Lord's direct revelation as well as God's faithfulness in caring for Elijah
over the last three-and-a-half years. Furthermore, Elijah's
faith was bolstered by God's response to his prayers.
Though Elijah's wilderness experience was often difficult,
filled with lonely days, sleepless nights, fearful moments,
and periods of doubt and uncertainty, he was now prepared
to face not only Ahab and the prophets of Baal and
Asherah, but all Israel. And that day he met the king he
wasted no time in issuing his challenge, "Now summon *the
people from all over Israel* to meet me on Mount Carmel.
And bring the four hundred and fifty prophets of Baal and
the four hundred prophets of Asherah, who eat at Jezebel's
table" (18:19).

God designed the dramatic contest that lay ahead not primarily for the false prophets but for the deluded people. The prophets of Baal and Asherah were to serve as a means in God's hand to demonstrate their false theology, their meaningless rituals, and their evil ways to the people of Israel. The Lord wanted them to see for themselves that they were being led astray.

AHAB'S ORDER
1 Kings 18:20

Ahab, thinking he could handle whatever Elijah had in mind, issued an order throughout Israel. We don't know how many people responded and climbed Mount Carmel, but it must have been a multitude. No doubt the order included enough information to arouse their curiosity. They knew something unusual was going to happen. In fact, the majority were probably highly motivated to come just to catch a glimpse of this prophet of God who was responsible for the drought that plagued Israel for three-and-a-half years. Some were probably angry, some confused and others just curious. They knew no doubt of Ahab's fruitless search for Elijah and how Elijah was going to appear on Mount Carmel. Little did they know that they were going to see not just a courageous old prophet but experience a demonstration of God's power that would affect their lives for years to come.

Mount Carmel was a perfect place for this contest. It was to serve as a great outdoor theater that would accommodate thousands of people. The "stage" was one of the largest in the world. It had to be, because it would need to accommodate nearly four hundred and fifty men who would perform at one time. In fact, it could accommodate nearly one thousand, though only the prophets of Baal responded to Ahab's order.

The specific location was at a place called *el-Mohraka*. Robert Jamieson, in his commentary on 1 Kings, graphically describes the setting:

> Mount Carmel is a bold, bluff promontory . . . It is a
> long range, presenting many summits and intersected
> by a number of small ravines. The spot where the con-
> test took place is situated at the eastern extremity,
> which is also the highest point of the whole ridge. It is
> called el-Mohraka, "the Burning," or "the Burnt
> Place." No spot could have been better adapted for the
> thousands of Israel to have stood, drawn up on those
> gentle slopes. The rock shoots up in an almost perpen-
> dicular wall of more than 200 feet in height . . . This
> wall made it visible over the whole plain, and from all
> its surrounding heights, where gazing multitudes
> would be stationed.[1]

ELIJAH'S CHALLENGE
1 Kings 18:21

When the people finally gathered, Elijah issued his challenge. Going before the people, he said, "How long will
you waver between two opinions? If the Lord is God, follow him; but if Baal is God, follow him" (1 Kings 18:21).

Elijah's question reveals a very important fact. There
were still two opinions among the children of Israel. The
majority probably still believed in the God of their fathers.
However, they had also been worshiping Baal and Asherah.

Asherah was identified as the goddess of sex and war.
Licentious worship was conducted in her honor. Jezebel's
father was a priest of Asherah, which helps explain her
intense involvement in this pagan religion.

Baal was identified as the farm god who gave increase
to the field. He was also identified with the storm god,
Hadad, whose voice could be heard in the reverberating
lightning and thunder that accompanied rain.

We can now understand more fully why God chose to
focus Elijah's confrontation on Baal. In fact, we can also

understand why God chose to judge Israel with a drought. The children of Israel were about to see that there was only *one God* who was in control of the elements—the God of Abraham, Isaac, and Jacob. Against this historical backdrop, Elijah's question becomes even more significant.

THE PEOPLE'S RESPONSE
1 Kings 18:21b

The latter part of verse 21 represents one of the most succinct but revealing statements in the Old Testament. We simply read, "But the people said nothing." Their response to Elijah's question was deafening silence! And in saying "nothing," they *were saying* several important things.

First, they didn't want to make a decision. Why choose? Why not worship both the God of their fathers as well as Baal? Why not include Asherah? Why be monotheistic? Could they not be polytheistic and "have their cake and eat it too"? After all, wasn't it a bit narrow to worship only one God?

Second, they were enjoying their worldly life-style. After all, the moral codes of Jehovah were demanding and very much out of harmony with the immoral code associated with pagan worship. Temple prostitution and all kinds of sexual immorality were an intricate part of their religious rituals, whereas God's standards condemned sexual promiscuity. It is always easier to follow the desires of the flesh than the will of God.

Third, they were no doubt afraid to voice an opinion, especially if they inclined towards worshiping the Lord God rather than Baal and Asherah. After all, the king and queen worshiped these pagan gods—Baal and Asherah. And there stood Ahab, who had called this public meeting in the first place. Silence was predictable. To speak up in this context would call for unusual courage and very strong conviction, and they had neither. It is not surprising that "the people said nothing."

Lot's Example (Gen. 19:1-26)

"Wavering between two opinions" is not a new phenomenon in either biblical history or history in general, or in our own personal experiences from day to day. In biblical history it is epitomized in the Old Testament story of Sodom and Gomorrah, two ancient cities that became so wicked that God eventually destroyed them. However, before judgment fell, the Lord responded to Abraham's concern for his nephew who lived in Sodom, and sent two angels to warn Lot and his family. Even then, Lot hesitated to leave. When he did, "the men grasped his hand and the hands of his wife and of his two daughters and led them safely out of the city" (Gen. 19:16). Had they not applied pressure, Lot and his family would have stayed in Sodom, ignoring God's warning of impending doom.

As soon as they had left the city, the angels warned them further, "Flee for your lives! Don't look back and don't stop anywhere in the plain. Flee to the mountains or you will be swept away!" (19:17).

Even then, "Lot's wife looked back" ignoring God's warning, "and she became a pillar of salt" (19:26). What happened exactly we do not know. Perhaps she lagged so far behind, not really wanting to leave "sin city" that she was caught in the storm of burning sulphur God rained down on Sodom and Gomorrah. Or perhaps it was God's eventual judgment on her for ignoring His warnings and His long-suffering and mercy. Whatever happened, Lot's wife brought this calamity on herself because she, like the children of Israel on Mount Carmel, wavered "between two opinions." How enticing and deceptive sin can be!

Joshua's Warning (Josh. 24:14-18)

Joshua, Moses' successor, recognized this weakness in the children of Israel. After they had occupied the land of Canaan and before he "sent the people away, each to his own inheritance" (Josh. 24:28), he issued a solemn warning as well as a personal witness. This is in fact the same question Elijah posed to the people on Mount Carmel, only in the form of an exhortation. "Choose for yourselves this day whom you will serve, whether the gods your forefathers served beyond the River, or the gods of the Amorites, in whose land you are living. But as for me and my household, we will serve the Lord" (24:15).

Even though the generation in Joshua's day responded positively, saying, "Far be it from us to forsake the Lord to serve other gods", (24:16) future generations violated this commitment. In fact, it happened very quickly, for we read that after Joshua's death, "another generation grew up . . . and served Baal and the Ashtoreths" (Judg. 2:10-13).

And so it happened generation after generation in Israel. But God in His mercy and patience again and again reached out to His people, as He was once again doing through Elijah on Mount Carmel. And once again He was saying, "How long will you waver between two opinions? If the Lord is God, follow him; but if Baal is God, follow him." Once more He was giving them another opportunity to follow the Lord.

When we review Old Testament history correctly we see a God of incredible patience and long-suffering. At the slightest response on the part of people to turn from their sins, He is quick to withdraw the judgments and to forgive them. True, at times His hand of judgment falls, but always after a very lengthy period of warnings and toleration of some of the most horrible and hideous atrocities and crimes. Pagan worship not only involved gross immorality, but often involved the murder of innocent people.

DOUBLE-MINDEDNESS AND THE TWENTIETH-CENTURY CHRISTIAN

Before we look specifically at Elijah's encounter with the prophets of Baal, we need to think seriously about Elijah's question. James gives a New Testament perspective when he wrote that a "double-minded man" is "unstable in all he does" (Jas. 1:7).

Every believer must look carefully at what happened to the children of Israel generation after generation. How quickly they departed from God's will and worshiped idols! How often they followed after their own fleshly desires! How easily they seemed to forget all that God had done for them! How hardened they became to the fact that they were bringing judgment not only on themselves but also on their children.

And so, Elijah's question comes ringing and echoing down through the centuries as it rang out that day on Mount Carmel and echoed and reverberated through the canyons and out into the open valleys and plains at the foot of Mount Carmel: "How long," he still cries, "will you waver between two opinions?"

To be double-minded usually means having one foot planted *firmly* on the soil of this world's system and the other planted *softly* in God's kingdom. We have not yet made that choice to follow Jesus Christ totally. Like Lot, someone has taken our hand and hesitantly we are following, but in our hearts we really "don't want to leave Sodom." Whether we've faced it or not, it is really where we want to stay. And some of us perhaps are like Lot's wife. We're reluctantly "walking away" but "looking back." And some of us are like the children of Israel. When Elijah posed that question they "said nothing."

Our reasons for double-mindedness are often similar to Israel's.

We don't want to make a decision. We're apathetic. The issue isn't that important to us. Furthermore, we don't want to be called fanatics. After all, we say, there are many ways to heaven. To believe in "one way" is a sign of ignorance, cultural deprivation, and bigotry.

We're enjoying our worldly life-style. This is not surprising, for the Scriptures identify sin as attractive. Moses struggled with that same decision for the same reasons we struggle. But, we read that "he chose to be mistreated along with the people of God rather than to enjoy the pleasures of sin for a short time" (Heb. 11:25).

But there is a key phrase in this scriptural statement. The "pleasures of sin" are short-lived! They never satisfy. We go from one experience to another but we're never fulfilled. It's subtle but true, whether people admit it or not.

All of us are tempted. Many times in my own life sin looks very attractive! It always does—and more so at a distance! The grass always seems greener on the other side of the fence and at times I find myself wavering, stopping and looking both ways, and even moving in the wrong direction.

Does that ever happen to you? These feelings and desires should not surprise us. They are normal and natural. But to yield leaves us guilty, unsatisfied and often brokenhearted. Ask any person who has yielded to Satan's wooing! Furthermore, read the Scriptures. They are filled with examples of people who failed God. We never need experience the result of sin to be convinced that it's a dead-end street. To learn by personal experience is a terrible price to pay, especially when we don't have to. Ask David, or Saul, or Solomon!

We are afraid to take a stand. Maybe our friends, or even parents, will make fun of us or reject us or withhold things from us. For most of us this may not be a severe problem. But if you were a Muslim you might be killed if you became a Christian. If you were from a strict Jewish home, you might be considered dead—and treated that way. And, if you were a part of some other religious group, you might be excommunicated.

At times I have shared some of my own religious background, but I have done so cautiously because I still have many dear friends and blood relatives who are still a part of the religious group in which I grew up. But, in conjunction with this message, I feel I must share part of that experience.

My parents were part of a very exclusive religious community. I grew up within this community, going to Sunday School and church regularly as a child. At age sixteen I became an official member of the group. Though I already had reservations about some of the doctrinal teachings, I still believed it represented the *best* of all religious communities.

However, after becoming a member of the church, I began to see things quite differently. Not only was I convinced that the leaders were teaching a number of doctrinal errors, but I saw little spiritual reality in the lives of many people. They were faithful church attenders, but their relationship with God and others was far from being consistent with what I read in Scripture.

Because of my concerns and desire to learn more, I began to attend youth and Bible conferences sponsored by other Christian organizations. Consequently, I began to learn, more than ever before, what the Bible teaches. I also began to listen to a Christian radio station coming from Moody Bible Institute in Chicago. Furthermore, through these experiences I was also motivated to study the Bible on my own.

Toward the end of my high school years I decided to apply to Moody Bible Institute where I could go and study the Bible more in depth. From the viewpoint of this religious group, this was my first major mistake. They disagreed with my decision. In fact, the leaders of the church were opposed to Bible study in the first place. And to study the Bible in a school of higher learning outside of my religious group was definitely a violation of their religious scruples.

My next major mistake, from their perspective, was to marry a girl who was not a part of this religious community. This represented an even greater departure from "the faith."

Understand it was not an issue with them of whether or not to marry a Christian or a non-Christian. It was an issue of marrying someone who was not a part of this religious group. To them, no one outside of this group could possibly be acceptable to God.

On the surface, and to an outsider, this experience may have appeared to be a minor religious episode in the life of a young person. However, it was a very difficult process lasting for several years. I had been brought up in this religious community. My parents were a part of this community. I had been indoctrinated in this religion and taught that we alone had religious truth. I'd also been taught that to associate with other people who claimed to be Christians would definitely jeopardize my chances of ever inheriting eternal life. In fact, when I was excommunicated, those who took actions against me definitely believed I had departed from the faith and was hopelessly lost. In fact, many of them still believe that to be true.

As a teenager I was terribly torn emotionally between what I had been taught and what I was learning from my study of Scripture. Though I saw definite contradictions, those cultural and emotional ties often overwhelmed me and caused me to waver. To face the prospect of being rejected by those I had been taught to respect as God's human representatives was a constant fear. Furthermore, I had developed some very deep friendships.

But eventually the decision was made. In some respects it was made for me. My parents were sympathetic and eventually made the same decision I made, but they also experienced deep emotional pain through the process. All of those factors combined to make this the most difficult period of my life.

But once the decision was made, the chains that bound me fell off. Though it took time to heal emotionally, I immediately experienced a new sense of freedom. I stopped wavering between two opinions. I knew what I believed, and the most wonderful part of the whole process was to know that I was saved, for I had been taught from a child that you really can't be sure of eternal life until you pass into that "great beyond." Perhaps, then, if you had been good enough and had attended church regularly and had been obedient to the elders, God might smile on you finally and welcome you to heaven. Perhaps this will help you understand why it was so difficult to take a stand against these leaders.

Fear of rejection is a strong deterrent in making any decision. But when it comes to following Christ, we must make the right decision. He must come first.

In this sense, the children of Israel surely were wavering between two opinions. To follow God and God alone would mean rejection by the majority of people in Israel. They were fearful to take a stand.

A PERSONAL RESPONSE

The following questions are designed to help all of us face Elijah's question honestly:

1. Am I double-minded? Am I wavering between two opinions?

2. Why am I double-minded?

NOTE: To follow Christ completely means giving Him control of everything—your family, your social life, your business, you bank account, etc.

3. In what specific ways am I double-minded?

4. Could it be I have never decided to follow Jesus Christ at all?

A SCRIPTURAL PRAYER OF COMMITMENT

Heavenly Father, today . . .

- I am going to serve only one Master, Jesus Christ the Lord (Matt. 6:24).
- I am going to continually seek first your kingdom and your righteousness (Matt. 6:33).

- I am going to deny myself and take up my cross daily and follow Jesus Christ (Mark 8:34).
- I now present my body to you and with your help I will renew my mind daily in order to conform my life to Christ's will (Rom. 12:1-2).

Note

1. Robert Jamieson, *A Commentary on the Old and New Testaments,* vol. 2 (Grand Rapids: Wm. B. Eerdmans Publishing Co., 1948), p. 353.

8

Putting God First

Elijah's initial challenge involved both "the four hundred and fifty prophets of Baal and the four hundred prophets of Asherah" (1 Kings 18:19). However, only the prophets of Baal responded to Ahab's order. It may be that Jezebel warned her prophets who ate at her table to avoid the confrontation. If so, she may have been simply ignoring Elijah's challenge. On the other hand, she may have actually been fearful of what might happen.

The facts are that neither Jezebel nor her prophets made an appearance. This could point to a disagreement between the king and the queen. Knowing Ahab, however, it would seem unlikely that he would respond to Elijah's challenge without Jezebel's approval. On the other hand, if Ahab acted on his own—as it appears he did—then, whatever the circumstances, it is reasonable to conclude that he was trying to prove to himself and his subjects that he could do something without Jezebel. And indeed he did! But he was soon to return to the queen with a story of embarrassing defeat (19:1).

ELIJAH'S PROPOSITION
1 Kings 18:22-25

Elijah made his proposition first to the children of Israel and then to the prophets of Baal. This is a significant sequence, for as stated in the last chapter, the demonstration on Mount Carmel was not for the benefit of the false prophets but rather for all Israel. This becomes clear in Elijah's proposal.

To the People (1 Kings 18:22-24)

Following the challenge and plea to those gathered on Mount Carmel to decide between God and Baal, and following their silent response indicating their refusal to make a decision (1 Kings 18:21), Elijah then issued his bold proposition. In essence, he told them he was only one prophet representing the Lord God among four hundred and fifty prophets who were representing Baal. This disparity, of course, was more than obvious, which was all a part of God's plan to prove His point.

Though it was four hundred and fifty to one, Elijah's proposal was the same as if it were based on a one-to-one ratio. He did not call for one representative from the prophets, as would normally be done in a duel or contest of this nature, yet he offered a plan that was the same as if there were total equality. "Get *two* bulls for us," he told the people (18:23). And going the extra mile, Elijah informed Israel that he would let the four hundred and fifty prophets have first choice, no doubt to eliminate any possibility of later being accused of some predetermined scheme.

Elijah's wisdom is also clear when he told *the people*— not the prophets—to choose the bulls. There would be no opportunity to accuse him of dishonesty or any form of trickery.

From this point on, the proposal involved the sacrifice itself. Again, to eliminate the possibility of being accused of some trick, Elijah gave the prophets first choice of which bull they wanted. Then, they were to cut it in pieces and lay it on a pile of wood. Elijah would do the same, but neither would set the wood on fire. Rather, both sides would call on their respective "gods"—they on Baal and he on the name of the Lord—and, "the god who answers by fire," Elijah continued, "he is God" (18:24).

At this point the people broke their silence. Though not overly enthusiastic, they were satisfied with Elijah's proposition. They actually had no choice. Their backs were against the wall. Clearly, it was more than fair. To reject Elijah's proposal would be in essence to admit that they were afraid to pit Baal against the Lord God. "What you say is good," they responded (18:24b).

To the Prophets (1 Kings 18:25)

After securing the approval of the children of Israel, Elijah then turned to the prophets. His proposal to them went a step further in giving them the edge. In fact, he was allowing them every opportunity to upstage him. "Choose one of the bulls and prepare it first," he said. However, you can't miss his sarcasm as he finished off his statement. "You go first," he quipped, "since there are so *many* of you."

Again, their backs were against the wall. Even if Elijah's sarcasm made them angry, to refuse would be to admit defeat before the contest began. Since Elijah's proposal was already so stacked in their favor, for them to make any alternate suggestions would certainly weaken their credibility in the eyes of the children of Israel.

THE PROPHETS' PRAYERS
1 Kings 18:26-29

The Scripture states that these men "called on the name of Baal from morning till noon" (1 Kings 18:26). They shouted! They danced! And later in the day they "slashed themselves with swords . . . until their blood flowed" (18:28). And "they continued their frantic prophesying until the time for the evening sacrifice" (18:29). All day long they prayed to Baal! But there was silence in heaven. There was no thunder, or lightning—and no fire! The Scriptures succinctly summarize what happened: "There was no response, no one answered, no one paid attention" (18:29).

Elijah's confidence in God, and at the same time his ability to use sarcasm, became very evident about noontime. He seemingly took a silent stance to this point. He then entered the scene and urged them to "shout louder!" Taunting them, he continued, "*Surely* he is a god! Perhaps he is deep in thought, or busy, or traveling. Maybe he is sleeping and must be awakened" (18:27).

With every statement and question Elijah revealed his knowledge of the false prophets' theology which taught that Baal at times was "deep in thought," or that at times he was on a journey, or that he was sleeping. Consequently, to urge them to "shout louder" reflected *their* way of getting Baal's attention.

There was a message, then, for the watching crowds in Elijah's sarcastic manner. If Baal was a god, why didn't he respond as they had been taught he would? Why wouldn't he listen? If what they believed about him was true, why would he not answer their prophets? After all, there were four hundred and fifty men shouting and dancing! Furthermore, they had been at it all morning.

Elijah's sarcasm was not a display or pride and arrogance. It played a very important part in making his point to Israel even more clear. And it worked. The prophets of Baal "shouted louder!" And they demonstrated their sincerity by being willing to injure themselves. And they continued their pagan ritual *all day long,* "until the time for the evening sacrifice" (18:29). This, of course, was all a part of Elijah's strategy—to eventually focus everyone's attention on God's laws regarding worship and sacrifice.

ELIJAH'S PREPARATION
1 Kings 18:30-35

The time had come. The prophets of Baal had failed. This was Elijah's moment. All eyes were on him. Had he gone first, there would have been no way to demonstrate the power of God against the backdrop of their total and utter failure to get Baal to respond.

Elijah also took his time. He asked the people to gather around and watch what he was going to do. First, "he repaired the altar of the Lord, which was in ruins" (1 Kings 18:30). The status of God's place of worship on Mount Carmel was evidence of Israel's idolatry. They no longer worshiped Him. In fact, they had no doubt destroyed the altar (1 Kings 19:10,14).

In repairing this altar, Elijah made another significant move. He "took twelve stones, one for each of the tribes descended from Jacob" (18:31), reminding the watching multitudes of their divine history. Though the biblical account gives no evidence of what Elijah might have said during this building process, it is difficult to imagine that he worked in silence. As he put each stone in place, he must have recounted God's marvelous grace in calling Israel out of Egypt and giving them an inheritance in Canaan.

In fact, he may have recounted the Lord's instructions to Joshua after Israel had miraculously crossed over Jordan. As Elijah put each stone in place, his conversation may have gone like: "Don't you remember what God did for our forefathers at the Jordan River? He backed up the water and they crossed over into Canaan on dry ground. And don't you remember what God told Joshua? He told them to choose twelve men from among the people, one from every tribe. Furthermore, He instructed Joshua to have these men take up twelve stones from the middle of the Jordan. And thus when our forefathers moved on to Gilgal, they set up those twelve stones as a memorial to the Lord.

"Do you know why they did that?" Elijah may have asked as he put another stone in place. "Let me tell you." Quoting Joshua he would have said: " 'In the future when your descendants ask their fathers, "What do these stones mean?" tell them, "Israel crossed the Jordan on dry ground. For the Lord your God dried up the Jordan before you until you had crossed over. The Lord your God did to the Jordan just what he had done to the Red Sea when he dried it up before us until we had crossed over. He did this so that all the peoples of the earth might know that the hand of the Lord is powerful and so that you might always fear the Lord your God" ' " (Josh. 4:21-24).

Though only a small number in the great multitude gathered on Mount Carmel would be able to see and hear, the word would have passed from person to person down through the valleys and out into the plains, which is all the more reason why Elijah would take his time.

His next moves were even more dramatic! To make sure Israel knew what was about to happen was no trick, "he dug a trench" around the altar (1 Kings 18:32). And after preparing the sacrifice, he asked the people themselves to pour water on the altar. Three times he had them fill "four large jars with water and pour it on the offering and on the wood" (1 Kings 18:33). In fact, there was so much water it filled the trench at the base of the altar (18:35).

Again, Elijah was demonstrating that what was about to happen was going to be a miracle from God. There was no way there could have been a "secret" fire burning under the altar. There was no way Elijah could use sleight of hand to start the fire himself, for wet wood and soaked meat cannot be ignited suddenly.

ELIJAH'S PRAYER
1 Kings 18:36-37

Elijah's plan, whatever time it took, coincided with the

"time of sacrifice." At that moment he "stepped forward and prayed." He didn't shout! He didn't dance! And he didn't cut himself! And as far as we know, he repeated the prayer only once. All in all, it took only a few seconds to say what he had to say. "O Lord, God of Abraham, Isaac and Israel, let it be known today that you are God in Israel and that I am your servant and have done all these things at your command. Answer me, O Lord, answer me, so these people will know that you, O Lord, are God, and that you are turning their hearts back again" (18:36-37).

There are a couple of points in this prayer that should be emphasized, *First, note the order in the following statement:* "Let it be known today that *you are God* in Israel and that *I am your servant*." Elijah made it crystal clear in his prayer that the purpose behind what was about to happen was to demonstrate that the *Lord was God*. Elijah was merely a human agent *serving* God. Furthermore, Elijah wanted Israel to know that whatever he was doing was not of his own making. God had spoken to him and the dramatic things that he had said and done were a result of God's command (18:36b).

Second, Elijah wanted Israel to know that the major reason God was about to demonstrate His power was to "turn their hearts back to Him." He was reaching out to them. He was demonstrating mercy, as He had done so many times before. He was faithfully keeping His promises to His faithless people.

GOD'S IRREFUTABLE PROOF
1 Kings 18:38

There is one thing that is clear in Scripture. When God wants people to know that He is speaking directly from heaven, He is far from subtle. His message is always clear. And so it was on Mount Carmel. He indeed offered irrefutable proof. Though the human stage had been set with twelve stones, the wood, a sacrifice—all drenched with water, God was now to add the divine dimension. We read that the "fire of the Lord fell and burned up the sacrifice" and "the wood." But the fire of God burned up not only the water-soaked logs, but "the stones and the soil and also licked up the water in the trench" (1 Kings 18:38).

Imagine the horror that must have been reflected in the faces of every observer. Fire that hot would have driven them back and away from the altar that once existed. Furthermore, there was a powerful message in this display of power—one they could not miss. In destroying the twelve stones, symbolic of the twelve tribes, God was saying that He was capable of destroying all Israel! Once again, God was warning His people of what would eventually happen if they continued to reject His love and mercy! But, more important, at this moment His message of judgment was also his message of love! He was giving them another opportunity to turn from their idolatry and sin and once again follow Him.

THE PEOPLE'S PROCLAMATION
1 Kings 18:39

God's message was loud and clear to Israel. They fell prostrate on the ground and cried, "The Lord, he is God! The Lord—he is God!" (1 Kings 18:39). How long they repeated this proclamation, we don't know. Considering the circumstances, those closest probably began the chant and those farther out joined them in the ever-widening circle of people shouting, "The Lord, he is God."

What a sight it must have been. And what a verbal demonstration must have reverberated through the valley for miles around.

What a contrast this was to the prolonged prayers and shouting of the prophets of Baal. They were shouting and asking for *proof* that Baal was God. The children of Israel were shouting a *proclamation* that the Lord *was* God! They had their proof!

THE PROPHETS' PUNISHMENT
1 Kings 18:40

God not only proved that He was God by sending fire from heaven, but His judgment fell on the prophets of Baal. At Elijah's command, the people themselves seized these evil men and executed them in the Kishon Valley (1 Kings 18:40).

There is also a message for all mankind in this tragic event in the lives of these false prophets. God's judgment will eventually fall on all those who deny Him. Though His mercy is great and His long-suffering beyond measure, there will come a day when unbelievers will be separated from God forever. The Scriptures teach that "the wages of sin is death" (Rom. 6:23). And the book of Revelation speaks of that day when all people who deny God and His Son, Jesus Christ, will be eternally punished and separated from God's presence (Rev. 20:7-14).

On the other hand, the Bible teaches that those who respond to God's love and grace will be saved. The same Scripture that teaches that "the wages of sin is death," also teaches that "the gift of God is eternal life through Jesus Christ our Lord."

GOD'S REVELATION IN PERSPECTIVE

There's one major truth that emerges from this dramatic Mount Carmel experience. God was reaching out to Israel. He wanted them to know that He was God and that He was their Source of life, both temporal and eternal. Elijah's prayer focuses this truth when he said, "Answer me, O Lord, answer me, so *these people* will know that you, O Lord, are God, and that you are turning their hearts back again" (18:37).

This major truth, however, is in essence the truth that emerges from the whole of Scripture. It is the main story line that flows through the Bible from Genesis to Revelation. The moment Adam and Eve sinned and became spiritually separated from God, the Lord began to reach out to them and all people with a plan of restoration. The children of Israel, of course, all through history have been a unique part of that plan.

To understand the real significance of what happened between Elijah and the prophets of Baal, we need a larger scriptural perspective. The facts are that there were three main time periods in biblical history when God revealed Himself to mankind directly and in a dramatic way. The first involved Moses, the second, Elijah, and the third, Jesus Christ. Interestingly, all of these events involved mountaintop experiences. God's first major revelation, combining who He was and what His will is for all people, happened on *Mount Sinai*. His second revelation, as we've seen, was on *Mount Carmel*. And His third revelation was on what has come to be called the *Mount of Transfiguration*.

The Mount Sinai experience, Exodus 19:16-20. When God, through Moses, led Israel out of Egypt He eventually brought them to Mount Sinai. It was there that, for the first time, He revealed His moral laws which are in essence spelled out in the Ten Commandments. However this revelation did not involve only words; it involved expressions of God's power which are identified as "signs" and "wonders" and "miracles."

Moses described these events in detail: "On the morning of the third day there was thunder and lightning, with a thick cloud over the mountain, and a very loud trumpet blast. Everyone in the camp trembled . . . . Mount Sinai was covered with smoke, because the Lord descended on it in fire. The smoke billowed up from it like smoke from a furnace, the whole mountain trembled violently, and the sound of the trumpet grew louder and louder" (Exod. 19:16,18-19).

It was in this context that "Moses spoke" to God and "God answered him." And God "called Moses to the top of the mountain" and revealed His laws (19:20).

One thing is very clear from the biblical record. God wanted Israel—and us—to *know for sure* it was He who was speaking. Consequently, He verified His message with a never-to-be-forgotten demonstration of His omnipotent power.

The Mount Carmel experience, 1 Kings 18:20-39. Against the backdrop of what happened at Mount Sinai, we can better understand what happened on Mount Carmel. Once again God was speaking. However, this time He was attempting to turn Israel's hearts back to His will and ways. They had departed from His laws, had forsaken Him and turned to Baal, a false god, who had no divine power whatsoever. And once again, God did not leave question marks in Israel's mind regarding who He was. He had clearly revealed His laws at Mount Sinai. At this point, the Lord was calling them back to obedience, but verifying once again with His supernatural power that He was indeed the almighty and living God.

The Mount of Transfiguration experience, Luke 9:28-36. The third great event marking God's efforts at reaching out to Israel as well as to all mankind involved His Son, Jesus Christ. This was indeed His greatest revelation of all! And it is succinctly illustrated on another mountaintop—the Mount of Transfiguration.

One day Jesus Christ ascended a mountain to pray, taking with Him three well-known apostles—Peter, James, and John. While Christ was praying, "the appearance of his face changed, and his clothes became as bright as a flash of lightning" (Luke 9:29). Furthermore, note that "*Moses* and *Elijah,* appeared in glorious splendor, talking with Jesus." The disciples, of course, were dumbfounded. And while Peter was verbally stumbling around trying to say something appropriate, "a cloud appeared and enveloped them . . . . A voice came from the cloud, saying, 'This is my Son, whom I have chosen; listen to him' " (9:34-35).

This supernatural event symbolized God's great and final revelation of Himself before Christ will come again, first to take all believers home to heaven and then to set up His kingdom on earth, leading to that great and final judgment.

This is one of the primary messages in the book of Hebrews which begins: "In the past God spoke to our forefathers through prophets at many times and in various ways, but in these last days he has spoken to us by his Son, whom he appointed heir of all things, and through whom he made the universe. The Son is a radiance of God's glory and the exact representation of his being, sustaining all things by his powerful word. After he had provided purification for sins, he sat down at the right hand of the Majesty in heaven" (Heb. 1:1-3).

A few paragraphs later, the author of this Hebrew letter adds a sobering warning: "We must pay more careful attention, therefore, to what we have heard . . . how shall we escape if we ignore such a great salvation? This salvation, which was first announced by the Lord, was confirmed to us by those who heard him. God also testified to it by signs, wonders and various miracles, and gifts of the Holy Spirit distributed according to his will" (Heb. 2:1-4).

With these very descriptive words, particularly in verse 4, the author of the Hebrew letter is telling us that God does not reveal Himself in subtle ways. On Mount Sinai He appeared in the context of lightning and thunder, fire and smoke, and a quaking mountain. At Mount Carmel He appeared in the fire that fell from heaven and destroyed not only the offering but the alter and the water in the trench. And when God revealed Himself through Jesus Christ and the apostles, He did so in the context of "signs, wonders and various miracles, and gifts of the Holy Spirit" (Heb. 2:4). He turned the water to wine, walked on the water, calmed the storm, healed blind people, cast out demons, and raised the dead. For all those who were willing to listen to Christ and the apostles, there was no question but that God was speaking.

Some have calculated that these three major events involving Moses, Elijah, and his successor, Elisha, and Jesus Christ and the apostles covered a total time span lasting no more than one hundred and fifty years. Generally speaking, these three brief time periods represent the "moments" in history when God revealed Himself in a special way, and verified His revelation with miraculous signs and wonders.

Some have defined the rest of the time—literally thousands of years—as periods known as God's "silent years." Not that God has not been present nor active in the affairs of mankind! Rather He was not speaking *directly* to men and women, accompanied with signs and wonders as He did through Moses, Elijah, and Elisha, and Christ and the apostles. In fact, nearly two thousand years have passed since God's last great revelation through His Son. And if the author of Hebrews is correct—and, of course, we believe he was—there will be no major manifestations of this nature until Jesus Christ comes again.

The next major dramatic event then is His coming. And when He comes, even those who have rejected God and His Son will someday bow the knee to Jesus Christ. Paul tells us that every tongue will "confess that Jesus Christ is Lord" (Phil. 2:11). Unfortunately, for many it will be too late to inherit eternal life, for they will bow out of force rather than out of freedom. They, along with Satan and his evil demons, will have to acknowledge that God is God! Satan, of course, acknowledges that even now, but he certainly has not bowed the knee.

However, we are still living in God's day of grace. His invitation is still available. We still have access to His long-suffering and mercy. In fact, Peter reminds us that He has not returned to judge the earth because "He is patient . . . not wanting anyone to perish, but everyone to come to repentance. But," Peter continues, "the day of the Lord *will come* like a thief. The heavens will disappear with a roar;

the elements will be destroyed by fire, and the earth and everything in it will be laid bare" (2 Pet. 3:9-10).

LIFE RESPONSE

God's will for all who read this chapter can be stated in the words of the author of the book of Hebrews: "Today, if you hear his voice, do not harden your hearts" (Heb. 3:7-8,15; 4:7).

This verse and challenge, of course applies whether we are Christians or not Christians! Let us bow our knee to God the Father, Jesus Christ His Son and the blessed Holy Spirit.

9

Overcoming Depression

Depression is not a unique human experience, even among God's choicest servants. Elijah certainly demonstrates this reality. What may be surprising is that Elijah's bout with depression came after his greatest spiritual victory. It was sudden with seemingly no warning. But in retrospect, it was predictable.

ELIJAH'S HIGH HOPES FOR ISRAEL
1 Kings 18:41-46

Following the Lord's great demonstration of power on Mount Carmel, Elijah had great hopes for revival in Israel. Understandably so! The people responded en masse, acknowledging that the Lord was the one true God. Their punitive actions against the prophets of Baal indicated their desire to turn from their idolatrous ways.

Most important, Elijah was encouraged by Ahab's response. The king's heart appeared to have become soft and humble before God. Imagine the scene. Following his utter defeat, Ahab's countenance must have reflected horrible dejection and weariness. Rather than condemning the king, Elijah encouraged him to return to his royal tent and regain his emotional and physical strength. "Go, eat and drink," Elijah said, "for there is the sound of a heavy rain" (1 Kings 18:41). In other words, Elijah was telling Ahab to cheer up! The drought was over. As he had told the king three and a half years ago, rain would come again.

What Elijah "heard" at that moment was, of course, in his heart. With the "ear of faith" he knew rain was on its way. At this point there were no visible clouds, no thunder, and no lightning. But Elijah knew there would be! His knowledge of God's will enabled him to "hear" things others could not hear. God had spoken, and the fire from heaven in answer to Elijah's prayer was just the beginning of what God had promised.

As Ahab "went off to eat and drink," Elijah once again made his way to the top of Mount Carmel to pray and wait for God to send rain. From that vantage point, he and his servant could look over the vast expanse of the Mediterranean. Seven times Elijah instructed his servant to climb to a lookout point to see if there was any evidence of the coming storm. And on the seventh time, the servant brought a positive report. "A cloud as small as a man's hand is rising from the sea," he said (18:44).

This was all the visible evidence Elijah needed. He instructed his servant to descend the mountain and to tell Ahab to hitch up his chariot and head for Jezreel before the rain became so intense it would be impossible to travel (18:44). And even before Elijah reached the valley below, "the sky grew black with clouds, the wind rose," and "a heavy rain" began to fall (18:45). At this juncture a very significant thing happened. As "Ahab rode off to Jezreel" in the blinding rainstorm, we read that "the power of the Lord came upon Elijah." He tucked "his cloak into his belt" and "ran ahead of Ahab all the way to Jezreel" (18:46).

What was happening? What is the purpose behind this rather strange behavior? First, Elijah was now an old man and the distance from Mount Carmel to Jezreel, where Ahab had his summer palace, was nearly twenty miles. This event, of course, represents another miracle. Humanly speaking, it was an impossible feat. The Lord was continuing to affirm to Ahab His presence and power through His servant Elijah.

Second, with God's help Elijah was demonstrating to Ahab that he was his servant and loyal subject. He had nothing personal against the king. His words of judgment that day three and a half years ago were meant to bring Israel back to God, King Ahab included.

Third, it was customary for the king to have a personal runner who would precede his chariot. Perhaps the designated runner had fled in the light of the shocking events that had just transpired on Mount Carmel. The mass execution of the prophets of Baal would have been reason enough to frighten people into hiding. Or, perhaps the coming storm sent him scurrying into some cave or makeshift shelter for protection from the elements.

Whatever the circumstances, Elijah became that runner. He who was greatest at that moment became Ahab's servant. Though the king could barely see through the blinding storm, he no doubt caught periodic glimpses of Elijah, head bowed low and his cloak flapping in the wind as he braved the elements and led the king's chariot over winding, muddy roads back to Jezreel.

The fourth reason Elijah ran ahead of Ahab's chariot relates to what Ahab would face when he returned to his palace. Jezebel would be waiting for a full report. He would need all the support he could get to stand up to this wicked woman and renounce her idolatry. Elijah was demonstrating his support, hoping Ahab would have the courage to not only share what happened, but to inform Jezebel that he must lead people back to God.

ELIJAH'S KEEN DISAPPOINTMENT AND DEPRESSION
1 Kings 19:1-4

Unfortunately, things did not turn out as Elijah had hoped. When Ahab reported on the Mount Carmel experience and that Elijah "had killed all the prophets [of Baal] with the sword," Jezebel was livid with anger (1 Kings 19:1)! Her wrath was too much for Ahab, and as always he faded into the woodwork. He did not stand up to his wicked queen.

You can imagine Elijah's keen disappointment when he received the following message from Jezebel: "May the gods deal with me, be it ever so severely, if by this time tomorrow I do not make your life like that of one of them" (19:2). Evidently Elijah was expecting a positive report that Jezebel had listened to Ahab, had decided to turn from her idolatry and humble herself before Almighty God. But not so! Like Pharaoh, king of Egypt, when he was faced with the manifestation of God's almighty power, she hardened her heart. She became more entrenched in her pagan ways and more steeped in her idolatry. Flying into a rage, she was determined to have Elijah killed!

At this point, there was an incredible change in Elijah's personality. In some respects, it's difficult to understand. His joy turned to sadness and his boldness to fear. We read that he "was afraid" of Jezebel's threats. Furthermore, he "ran for his life" (19:3).

As angry as Jezebel was, she did not lose complete rationality. She knew that to have Elijah killed would put her own life in danger. The children of Israel had responded positively to Elijah's victory over the prophets of Baal. The people themselves had executed these evil men. And though the prophets of Asherah had survived the ordeal by not responding to Ahab's order to appear on Mount Carmel, Jezebel knew she needed to proceed cautiously. Emotions were running high! Therefore, she gave Elijah a way out. In other words, she was telling him to get out of the country and stay out. Furthermore, she was giving him twenty-four hours, no doubt hoping he would do exactly what he did—run for his life.

What is amazing is that Elijah responded with intense fear! After facing four hundred and fifty prophets of Baal, he was now running from one woman! Was not God able to protect him from Jezebel, evil as she was? Somehow Elijah lost perspective and entered a state of deep depression. More than anything else, these events must have been what James had in mind when he identified Elijah as a "man just like us." The King James translation is even more literal and accurate. We read that he "was a man subject to like passions [of like feeling] as we are" (Jas. 5:17).

Elijah's depression was so severe that he wanted to die! In fact, he "*prayed* that he might die." Pouring out his soul before God, he said, "I have had enough, Lord . . . . Take my life" (19:4). Incidentally, God answered many of Elijah's prayers, but this one He did not answer directly. However, God responded and did what was best for Elijah.

ELIJAH'S EMOTIONAL HEALING BEGINS
1 Kings 19:5-9

In his state of depression, Elijah found a tree in the wilderness, lay down, and fell sound asleep (1 Kings 19:5). How long he slept, we're not told. But suddenly, he was awakened by an angel of the Lord who instructed him to "get up and eat." As he looked around, "there by his head was a cake of bread baked over hot coals, and a jar of water" (19:6).

Though Elijah's depression was severe, it didn't affect his appetite. "He ate and drank and then lay down again." And eventually the angel returned and awakened him the second time and gave him the same instructions. Once again Elijah dined under a broom tree in the wilderness.

Gradually Elijah's physical strength was restored, though, as we will see in our next chapter, it took more than food and rest to bring emotional healing to Elijah's soul. But he *was* strengthened. We read that "he traveled forty days and forty nights until he reached Horeb, the mountain of God." There he found a cave and entered and "spent the night" (19:8-9).

SOME IMPORTANT OBSERVATIONS ABOUT ELIJAH'S EXPERIENCE

To this point in time, we've focused on Elijah's great spiritual strengths—his boldness and courage, his faith in God, and his obedience in doing the will of God. Though we've observed his human weaknesses, such as his frustration when the widow's son died, we see in this lesson his most severe problem. He became so depressed he no longer wanted to live. Though he may not have contemplated suicide, he was experiencing the very same emotions that often drive people to take their lives. There is a fine line between thinking about suicide as a way to die and asking God to take away your life. Either way, Elijah was walking that line. He was in the depths of despair.

What causes depression? Elijah illustrates several common reasons.

First, depression often follows "mountaintop experiences." Elijah illustrates this point symbolically and literally. It so happens that his emotional highs took place on the top of Mount Carmel. Imagine the excitement and joy that must have flooded his soul when God responded to his prayers and sent fire from heaven. For three and a half years he had been waiting for this moment. The prolonged buildup alone would have generated unusual psychological reactions.

Mark it well! When we experience emotional highs we'll also experience emotional lows. It is a predictable pattern in human behavior.

Second, depression often follows intense periods of stress and hyperactivity. Though Elijah's emotions must have peaked on Mount Carmel, he also endured unusual stress as he confronted the prophets of Baal. Though he knew in his heart that God would answer his prayers and prove Himself victorious, he experienced all of the physiological changes that accompany this kind of emotional wear and tear. Adrenalin poured into his veins, and although God had granted him unusual strength in running a twenty-mile marathon in a blinding rainstorm, he was also drawing on his natural resources. And when we do, we'll eventually experience a low point, both physically and emotionally.

All of us have physical alarm systems that are activated under stress. It is this system that gives us unusual strength to go without sleep, to accomplish superhuman tasks, and to concentrate beyond our normal abilities. But, eventually our physiological systems return to normal. And when they do, depression is predictable. Certainly this *human* dynamic contributed to Elijah's sudden personality change even though his burst of energy was supernatural.

Third, depression often coincides with physical and emotional exhaustion. This factor is intricately related to the one just stated. Hyperactivity and stress certainly contribute to physical and emotional exhaustion.

God has created the normal human being to function within certain physiological and psychological boundaries. When we extend these boundaries unnecessarily, we are going to suffer the consequences. And unless we recreate and recuperate, we'll not rebound properly.

Following Elijah's stressful experience on Mount Carmel, he was exhausted. He was far beyond any human being's normal boundaries, and when threatened by Jezebel, he did not have enough human resources to go on. Consequently, he ran from the problem. What he was ordinarily able to cope with emotionally, he could no longer handle. In fact, his encounter with Jezebel was minor compared with his previous encounters with Ahab, the children of Israel, and the prophets of Baal. In fact, he was not even able to discern adequately that Jezebel's threats reflected her own fear of retaliation. Why could he not believe that God could protect him from this wicked woman? One answer is his physical and emotional exhaustion.

Fourth, depression often follows keen disappointment and disillusionment. Elijah had high hopes for national repentance in Israel. Most important, he was excited about Ahab's initial response. He did all he could to reassure the king of his loyal support. After all, he became his servant and ran ahead of the king's chariot all the way back to the palace. And, of course, he was hopeful that Ahab would take charge of the spiritual affairs of Israel and confront Jezebel.

But it didn't happen! Elijah's hopes and expectations were dashed. He was disillusioned and disappointed. In the midst of physical exhaustion, he dropped over the edge psychologically.

Fifth, depression often results from periods of anger, particularly if we don't deal with it properly. Was Elijah's depression related to deep feelings of anger? Probably! He *was* "a man just like us." After all, he had given himself totally to vindicate God's name. He had done his dead-level best to encourage Ahab to take a similar stand. And he had high hopes. But he knew there would be no significant and permanent change in Israel's behavior if the king himself did not change.

Under these circumstances anger would be a predictable response. And it certainly would contribute to Elijah's depression. It always does, particularly if it becomes a lingering response.

PRACTICAL LESSONS FROM ELIJAH'S EXPERIENCE

1. Being a dedicated Christian who is used of God in

significant ways does not guarantee that we'll not experience depression. Like Elijah, we're all human. We have our
physical and psychological limits. If we violate these limits
on a prolonged basis, we'll experience the consequences.

This does not mean we are unspiritual. And it does not
mean we will not be called upon to violate these limits. In
fact, the normal demands of life often force us into these
situations. Making a living, academic pursuits, parenting
and other domestic responsibilities often push us beyond
our normal boundaries. And ministry responsibilities are
even more demanding. This is why God created us with
"alarm systems."

The important point to remember is that depression does
not necessarily mean that we are out of fellowship with
God. The very fact that we recognize that truth enables us
to deal with depression and ride it through without intensi-
fying the problem by feeling guilty.

2. **Under certain circumstances we should expect
depression and its accompanying results.** When we face
"mountaintop experiences" emotionally, and when we find
ourselves in the midst of intense periods of stress and
hyperactivity, we should be prepared to face the consequences. Eventually we'll face a low point emotionally.
This is particularly true if we have used up our physical and
emotional reserves and have become exhausted.

We must remember also that disillusionment and disappointment cause depression. And since these factors are a
part of life, we should be prepared for the results. It is normal to experience periodic low points.

3. **Depression always distorts our view of reality.** When
Jezebel threatened Elijah's life he lost perspective. Though
he could certainly *recall* the specific events that had transpired on Mount Carmel and the ravine below, he could not
remember emotionally. In fact, at that moment, he seemingly could not draw strength from God's past faithfulness.
God's supernatural provisions in the valley of Kerith and in

the home of the widow were somehow beyond his psychological reach.

This should not surprise us. Depression thwarts our emotional memories and blurs our view of reality. God's acts of faithfulness in the past tend to lose their motivational effectiveness, and the present events causing our depression are totally distorted. Little problems appear huge and gigantic. Simple difficulties seem terribly complex. Temporary struggles appear endless. There seems to be no light at the end of the tunnel.

4. We must get sufficient rest and relaxation. If we do not, we're heading for trouble. There are times we are called upon to exert unusual amounts of physical and emotional energy. But if we do not take time to rest, eventually we'll lose ground and our efforts become counterproductive.

The story is told of two men who started a journey across the great northland with two dog teams. One man decided to stop and rest his dogs every seventh day. The other decided to drive straight through.

At the end of the first week of travel, the first man, as planned, stopped his team and rested all that day. The other man continued to travel. By the end of the next week, the man who had rested his dogs, nearly caught up with the man who traveled straight through. But again, the first man stopped to rest his team on the seventh day.

By the end of the third week, the man who had rested his team had passed the man who traveled straight through, and in the end reached the final destination far ahead of him.

Inherent in God's physical, emotional, and spiritual laws for mankind is the need for rest. Though we are not under Old Testament law, the principles are still applicable. Experience verifies it.

5. We are more vulnerable to satanic attacks when we are physically and psychologically exhausted. It is not by

accident that Satan tempted Christ in the wilderness *after* he had fasted for forty days and nights. Jesus was hungry and weak. It was then Satan made his move (Matt 4:1-11)! It should not surprise us then that Satan strikes us when we are weak. Consequently, we must be on guard during these periods of stress.

6. Knowing these things about depression will in themselves help us to cope with its presence and its affects in our lives. Nothing complicates depressive moods more than worry. It only accentuates the problem and intensifies the anxiety that may have caused it in the first place. Consequently, accepting depression as a reality helps to overcome it, realizing there are reasons for its existence at this moment in our lives.

As we'll see, however, Elijah needed more than food and rest. But it is significant that this is where the Lord began in the healing process. And normally, this is where we must begin as well.

LIFE RESPONSE

1. Using both the observations about Elijah's experience and the lessons he teaches us as a checklist for your own life, can you isolate the causes for depression in your own life? What steps do you need to take to care for this problem?

2. Think of someone who is suffering from lingering depression. Share the message of this chapter with him for comfort and encouragement.

10

God's Counseling Procedures

The Lord's initial step in helping Elijah to overcome his depression was to help him recuperate physically. How much time elapsed while he ate and slept in the wilderness of Beersheba, we don't know. But following his second meal, Elijah "traveled forty days and forty nights until he reached Horeb, the mountain of God" (1 Kings 19:8).

Often when we study this passage, which deals with Elijah's depression, we stop with the statement that he was strengthened by the food and "traveled forty days and forty nights" assuming his psychological problems were solved. In fact, I have been guilty of that conclusion myself. Unfortunately, that is not the case.

Our first clue that Elijah continued in his depressed state relates to how long it took him to make the trip from Beersheba to Horeb. The total distance is about two hundred miles. Elijah, then, took his time, averaging only five miles a day. Had he been emotionally motivated, he could have made the trip in a week.

What a contrast between the man who ran twenty miles ahead of Ahab's chariot from Mount Carmel to Jezreel, and the man who is now trudging through the wilderness headed for Mount Horeb, no doubt looking as if he had the weight of the world on his shoulders. Previously he had been buoyed up with excitement and anticipation. Now, he was burdened down with sadness and a heavy heart. Though he had been strengthened physically from the food and rest in Beersheba, he was still emotionally down. His depression had not subsided.

COUNSELING SESSION I
1 Kings 19:9-12

When Elijah arrived at Horeb, he went into a cave and spent the night. And while there, God once again spoke to him.

The Lord's Question (1 Kings 19:9)

"What are you doing here, Elijah?" the Lord asked.

Elijah's Answer (1 Kings 19:10)

"I have been very zealous for the Lord God Almighty. The Israelites have rejected your covenant, broken down your altars, and put your prophets to death with the sword. I am the only one left, and now they are trying to kill me too."

The old prophet's response once again reflected his emotional exhaustion and his inability to cope with the demands of life. It *was* true that he had been "zealous for the Lord God Almighty." He *had* boldly confronted Ahab regarding the coming drought. He *had* been faithful to God during the long, lonely period of waiting in the ravine of Kerith. He *had* laid his own reputation on the line when he prayed for the widow's son to be restored to life. He *had* obeyed God's charge to meet Ahab and the false prophets on Mount Carmel. And there he followed through with everything God told him to do. Indeed, Elijah had "been *very* zealous for the Lord God Almighty." No one could deny that reality.

Furthermore, it was also true that Israel had rejected God's covenant, had broken down the Lord's altars, and had put the Lord's prophets to death. These were stern realities!

But there were other realities he could not "see" or recognize. Israel had responded positively on Mount Carmel. Furthermore, it was not true that he was "the only one left who had not forsaken the Lord." What about his friend, Obadiah? And what about the one hundred prophets of the Lord whom Obadiah had hidden in the two caves?

Elijah's response illustrates another mental and emotional phenomenon associated with severe depression. Negative reality blocks out positive reality. All we tend to see are the facts that discourage us. The facts that should be encouraging elude us. Elijah's experience verifies this. He was so depressed he could not see beyond the dark clouds of despair that shrouded his weary soul.

What was God doing for Elijah? Food and rest brought physical strength. But Elijah also needed an opportunity to share how he felt, openly and honestly, without being judged and put down. This seems to be a primary reason the Lord asked him the question, "What are you doing here, Elijah?" (19:9). God knew, of course, what was in his heart. But he needed an opportunity to verbalize it, to get it out in the open.

The Lord's Counsel (1 Kings 19:11-13a)

Ventilation, per se, was not sufficient. Had it been a simple downer, it would have worked. Elijah's problem was too complex. He needed both spiritual and psychological insight. In fact, he needed some theological input and clarification. Thus the Lord told him to come out of the cave, to "stand on the mountain in the presence of the Lord, for the

Lord is about to pass by" (1 Kings 19:11).

What happened first was terrifying. God unleashed the fury of a "great and powerful wind." It was so strong it literally tore up the mountain, no doubt uprooting trees. Huge rocks cascaded down the mountain as if they were pebbles. "But," we read, "the Lord was not in the wind" (19:11). That is, God was not speaking as He had done at Mount Sinai.

Next, the Lord sent an earthquake. It must have been similar to God's presence on Mount Sinai years before when "the whole mountain trembled violently" (Exod. 19:18). But again we read that "the Lord was not in the earthquake" (1 Kings 19:11c).

Next, the Lord sent a great fire, reminiscent of what God had just done on Mount Carmel in response to Elijah's prayer. But again we read that "the Lord was not in the fire" (19:12a).

Where then was the presence of the Lord? If He was not in the wind, the earthquake, or the fire, where was He? As the omnipotent and omnipresent God He was there, of course. In fact, He was speaking to Elijah. What we see is that God's abiding presence appeared now as "a gentle whisper" or a quiet rustling (19:12b).

COUNSELING SESSION II
1 Kings 19:13-18

The Lord's Question (1 Kings 19:13b)

Following this amazing demonstration of God's power, as well as His unique presence in the gentle, whispering wind, the Lord once again repeated His question, "What are you doing here, Elijah?"

Elijah's Answer (1 Kings 19:14)

"I have been very zealous for the Lord God Almighty. The Israelites have rejected your covenant, broken down your altars, and put your prophets to death with the sword. I am the only one left, and now they are trying to kill me too."

God's second question was identical to His first one. And so was Elijah's response. There was no outward evidence of any inward change. Depression and self-preoccupation continued to dominate both Elijah's attitudes and his actions. In fact, it appears God's command to "go and stand on the mountain" made little impact on Elijah. He even hesitated to come out of the cave as God had commanded.

Again, what a contrast! With every previously recorded command, Elijah was quick to obey God's will. Now, he hovered in the cave on Mount Horeb, making his appearance at the mouth of the cave only after God shook the landscape (1 Kings 19:13).

But God continued to patiently minister to and communicate with Elijah. Once again He gave Elijah an opportunity to ventilate his feelings.

The Lord's Counsel (1 Kings 19:15-18)

The Lord took another step in counseling Elijah. His next response was designated to help this servant get in touch with reality as well as his feelings. First, God told Elijah he was not alone. He was *not* the only prophet left, nor was he the only person who was still worshiping the one true God. Using round numbers, the Lord became very specific. There are "seven thousand in Israel—" the Lord said, "*all* whose knees have not bowed down to Baal" (1 Kings 19:18). In other words, God was saying to Elijah, "You are *not* the only one left!"

Furthermore, God told Elijah He never expected him to bear Israel's problems all alone. There are other men who would help—Hazael and Jehu and a man who was to have a very special place in Elijah's life—his successor, Elisha (19:15-17).

TO THIS POINT, HOW HAD GOD TREATED ELIJAH'S DEPRESSION?

First, He restored him physically. As human beings we must realize that God created us with various aspects to our personalities. We are physical beings; we are psychological beings; and we are spiritual beings. And these three dimensions are intricately interrelated. When we are not well *physically,* it affects us psychologically and spiritually. When we are experiencing *psychological* stress, it also affects us physically and spiritually. And when we are having *spiritual* problems, it affects the physical and psychological dimensions of our personalities.

In Elijah's situation all of these factors were interrelated. He was definitely exhausted physically. His psychological stress was overwhelming. Consequently, he lost his spiritual and theological perspective as well.

Interestingly, God began the process of healing by restoring him physically. And this is where we should begin if we are suffering from bouts with depression—or for that matter, any emotional distress. Though this may not be the major cause of our problem, it is always the place to begin, for it very well may be the basic cause. And even if it is not, it is easier to dissipate psychological stress if we are physically healthy.

NOTE: Medical doctors have discovered that some depression is caused by physical problems. In some instances, the problem is triggered by psychological stress and persists as a physically oriented problem. If this is true, this kind of depression must be treated medically as well as psychologically.

Second, God allowed Elijah to ventilate his feelings in a nonjudgmental setting. This is often a very important, necessary step in overcoming depression. When we are suffering from this emotional malady, we need to be able to share our feelings openly and honestly (but responsibly) without being judged or rejected. Feeling accepted by someone we trust, in spite of how we feel in itself, can often dissipate feelings of anxiety and depression.

As Christians we must believe that God always has a listening ear. He understands and He cares. And He is not ready to pounce on us and condemn us when we share our feelings with Him—negative though they may be. If this were His response, He would not wait until we share our feelings because He already knows what they are.

However, as human beings we need someone who not only will listen but will interact with us. Elijah, because of his relationship with God, experienced that interaction. God actually spoke to him, first in the context of acceptance, and second, by providing him with theological input.

We too need to ventilate our feelings with someone who listens nonjudgmentally, but who can help us gain both psychological and spiritual insight. And if the problem is severe and persistent, we no doubt need someone trained professionally, but preferably a Christian.

WARNING: Ventilation, per se, does not solve psychological difficulties. Furthermore, irresponsible and childish expressions of anger and frustrations do not solve these problems. To be specific we do not have to stomp our feet, scream, and use foul language to express psychological distress—no matter how severe it may be. We can pour out our feelings openly, honestly—but responsibly—just as Elijah did.

Third, God helped Elijah face reality. Some of Elijah's observations were accurate, and some were not. And it was those that were not accurate that were contributing significantly to his depression. Elijah needed to hear the facts that were eluding him. God firmly but lovingly communicated those facts.

It's important to know, however, that God didn't instruct Elijah until He had first given His servant opportunity to ventilate his feelings, not once, but twice. This initially helped him develop objectivity. But note also that

God did not wait for Elijah to repeat himself over and over again before He set the record straight.

This is important! Persistent verbal repetition does not solve emotional problems. In fact, if we repeat inaccuracies frequently, we only convince ourselves we're right and tend to entrench ourselves in our unreal world. There comes a time when we must stop verbalizing, listen, and then act on what is reality.

NOTE: If you're going to a counselor who time after time listens to you repeat your problems without correcting your point of view, you are wasting your time! And if you're paying for the service, you're wasting your money!

Fourth, God helped Elijah clarify his theological perspective. This point is not sequential. Intricately interwoven into the fabric of God's counseling process thus far were the theological lessons that God was teaching Elijah—lessons that were helping him maintain his spiritual and emotional equilibrium. What were those lessons?

• God's normal ways of communicating with His children are not *revelational* and oriented towards the dramatic and phenomenal. This theological lesson *focuses on God Himself.* More specifically, Elijah was learning that windstorms, earthquakes, and lightning bolts are not God's normal ways of revealing Himself. It is true that God always maintains sovereign control over all natural phenomena. But it is also true that God doesn't always speak directly through these natural upheavals and reveal His presence as He did at Mount Sinai, on Mount Carmel, and as He will surely do when His judgments fall on the earth in the great Tribulation period that will someday come on the earth (Rev. 6:12-14; 8:1-9).

God was teaching Elijah that His normal ways of revealing Himself are in a gentle, quiet way. In fact, He is *always* present in this way. And this was one of the theological lessons God was teaching His servant—and us!

• God's normal ways of relating to His children are *not*

extensively *experiential*. This theological lesson *focuses on man*. More specifically, it focuses on Elijah's religious experience. Understandably, this old prophet had come to expect the dramatic, the miraculous, the phenomenal! He experienced the three-and-one-half-year drought. He was miraculously fed by the ravens who brought him bread and meat every morning and every evening. He saw the jug of oil and the jar of meal never run dry. He prayed and the widow's son was restored to life. And most dramatic of all, he prayed and fire fell from heaven on the sacrifice of Mount Carmel, and later he saw the terrifying winds and the torrential rains that descended on the land of Israel.

There is no question that God was present and speaking in a specific way through all of these supernatural events. Elijah, being "a man just like us" had come to depend upon those "emotionally moving" experiences to affirm God's presence in his life and ministry.

But as we noted in chapter 8 God has not revealed Himself in this way during most of man's sojourn on earth. Thousands of years have passed when God's presence is sensed and felt, not in the wind, the earthquake and fire, but as a "gentle whisper."

• God's normal ways of dealing with His children are *not* with persistent external judgments. This third theological lesson *focuses on mankind in general* and *God's grace*. Periodically throughout history, His hand of judgment and punishment has fallen, but never until His patience has been pushed to the limits and even then God has been quick to relent if there was repentance.

Some Bible commentators believe Elijah's anger had taken over after the Mount Carmel experience, leaving him internally disturbed over the fact that God continued to tolerate Israel's idolatry and sinful behavior. If so, God was teaching Elijah that His ways are gentle and long-suffering; not bombastic and given to quick judgments and punishment for sin. Whether or not this is what God was teaching

Elijah at this time, it is certainly evident that God *is* long-suffering (2 Pet. 3:7-9).

• God is never dependent on one person alone to accomplish His goals. This lesson *focuses on God's appointed leaders*. No man is strong enough physically, psychologically or spiritually to handle God's work alone. Elijah needed to learn that lesson.

It's understandable why Elijah fell into this trap. After all, God had placed a heavy burden on his shoulders. In many respects, he had to stand alone during a three-and-one-half-year drought. But even then, there was Obadiah—and others who had stood true.

Throughout biblical history we observe this reality. Moses needed an Aaron, and later a Joshua. Paul needed a Barnabas, and later a Timothy and a Titus. Peter needed John. And as we'll see in our next chapter, Elijah needed an Elisha.

God's fourth theological lesson leads to the conclusion that God never expects one man or woman to bear the complete burden of any ministry. For that matter, God does not even expect any one of His children to live the Christian life in isolation. We need other Christians in our lives to encourage and help us.

SOME PERSONAL QUESTIONS

1. To the best of my ability, am I keeping myself in good physical condition—eating right, getting enough rest, exercise, etc.? When was the last time I had a complete and thorough physical examination?

2. Do I have someone with whom I can share my anxieties and frustrations without feeling judged? And when I share my feelings, do I do so in an open but responsible way?

3. Does the person I share with help me face reality? Do I *let* that person help me face reality? In other words, can I listen to advice as well as share my concerns?

4. Do I have a correct theological perspective on my personal problems?

- Am I waiting for God to speak to me in some unique way when He has already spoken through His Word and through my Christian friends and personal circumstances?

- Am I relying too much upon experience in my Christian life, expecting the abnormal, the miraculous, the unusual? Am I relying more upon my feelings than correct doctrine and biblical truth?

- Do I allow myself to get overly involved emotionally in other people's failures and problems, causing depression in my own life?

- Am I taking too much responsibility on myself, not realizing that God expects me to function only within the bounds of my human limitations—and that beyond this, God is ultimately responsible and in control?

11

The Importance of Friends

An English publication offered a prize for the best definition of a friend, and among the thousands of answers received were the following:

"One who multiplies joys, divides grief."

"One who understands our silence."

"A volume of sympathy bound in cloth."

"A watch which beats true for all time and never runs down."

But here is the definition that won the prize: "A friend—the one who comes in when the whole world has gone out."

If Elijah were here today to personally describe what happened following his mountaintop experience on Mount Carmel, he would surely agree with the definition that won the prize. However, he might paraphrase it this way: "When my whole world turned black as midnight, God brought Elisha into my life to be my friend." This indeed was God's final step in helping Elijah overcome his depression. This is the major focus in the passages we want to look at in this chapter.

But first, let's review. To this point, God has dealt with Elijah's depression in four very practical ways.

First, He ministered to him physically with food and rest.

Second, He gave Elijah the opportunity to ventilate his feelings in a nonjudgmental setting.

Third, God helped His faithful prophet face reality—to get his facts straight.

Fourth, He clarified his theological perspective.

There is yet a fifth step in God's counseling process when He dealt with Elijah's depression, one that is the most practical of all. He provided His servant with a companion whose name was Elisha.

A FAITHFUL ATTENDANT
1 Kings 19:12-21

God had already mentioned Elisha by name as being one of the men He had chosen to speak out against Israel's sin (1 Kings 19:17). But God's purpose in choosing this man was more than prophetic in nature. He was to serve alongside Elijah as his faithful attendant (19:21).

We're not sure how much God said to Elijah regarding the process of choosing Elisha. We're simply told that when he left Mount Horeb, he "went from there and found Elisha, son of Shaphat" (19:19).

Elisha lived in the Jordan valley, far north and east of Mount Horeb, in a place called Abel Meholah (19:16). His father was a farmer—no doubt a very well-to-do farmer. When Elijah found Elisha, he was working with eleven other men, each plowing with a yoke of oxen.

When Elijah suddenly appeared on the scene, Elisha no doubt knew who he was. Most everybody in Israel had heard about this feisty old prophet who had confronted Ahab and the prophets of Baal on Mount Carmel.

When Elijah saw Elisha, who was driving the twelfth

pair of oxen, he knew this was the man who was to become his attendant and eventually his successor. And when Elijah "threw his cloak around him," Elisha knew, through this symbolic act, that God had called him to be a special helper and assistant to this great prophet in Israel. He did not hesitate to leave his duties and his family to assist Elijah. To make sure everyone knew his commitment to this high task to serve both God and Elijah, he slaughtered his yoke of oxen and used his plowing equipment to cook the meat. He then invited his friends, neighbors, and fellow workers to join him in a farewell feast.

With this act of commitment, Elisha literally burned his bridges behind him. In his heart he was totally committed to Elijah and the God they both served. There was no turning back—and no conflict of interest.

Anyone who has faced a difficult task that is overwhelming, and in the process been able to recruit a qualified assistant, knows especially what it means to one's personal well-being—physically, psychologically, and spiritually. Part of God's healing process for Elijah's depression involved this very thing. He provided Elijah with a dedicated and faithful man who could help him carry the burden.

How long this Old Testament dynamic duo traveled and ministered together, we don't know. But one thing seems clear from the rest of the biblical account. Elijah's depression subsided when Elisha became his attendant. His activities, which are recorded in the first chapter of 2 Kings, reveal a man we knew *prior* to his bout with depression. He was once again responding to God's commands, and confronting the sins of idolatry at high levels in Israel (2 Kings 1:3-4).Once again, he was demonstrating God's power through miracles (1:10-14), and serving as God's instrument to bring judgment on Israel's leaders because of their failure to turn to God. Elijah's bout with depression was behind him.

But Elisha became more than Elijah's attendant. This is very evident in our next passage.

A LOYAL FRIEND
2 Kings 2:1-6

The time came when Elijah's work on earth was finished. But rather than let His servant die a natural death, the Lord decided to take him home to glory—"in a whirlwind" (2 Kings 2:1). Elijah's home-going was as dramatic as many events in his life!

Elisha made a statement to Elijah that is recorded three times in this passage. What he said communicates volumes regarding the relationship that had developed between these two men. When Elijah planned to visit a group of prophets on three different occasions in three different locations, he asked Elisha to stay behind. We're not sure of Elijah's motivation in issuing these commands. Perhaps it was because he knew his time was short and he didn't want to worry his friend. However, Elisha would not hear of it. Their dialog is summarized as follows:

ELIJAH'S COMMANDS	*ELISHA'S RESPONSES*
"Stay here; the Lord has sent me to Bethel" (2:2a).	"I will not leave you" (2:2b).
"Stay here, Elisha; the Lord has sent me to Jericho" (2:4a).	"I will not leave you" (2:4b).
"Stay here; the Lord has sent me to the Jordan" (2:6a).	"I will not leave you" (2:6b).

Elisha was not only Elijah's faithful attendant, he had become his loyal friend. In his heart he knew Elijah was about to leave him and he was determined to stay by his side until that moment when they would be separated.

There is a proverb that reads, "A friend loves at all times" (Prov. 17:17). And Jesus once said to His disciples just before He endured the cross, "Greater love has no one than this, that one lay down his life for his friends . . . . I no longer call you servants, because a servant does not know his master's business. Instead, I have called you friends, for everything that I learned from my Father I have made known to you" (John 15:13-15).

The disciples were called to be servants of Jesus Christ. But as they worked together, ate together, and shared many other experiences on earth, they developed a deeper and more meaningful relationship than merely "master and servant." They became *friends*. Jesus had shared with them the most intimate details of His life and His purpose on earth. They now knew "His business."

It's clear that Elisha developed this kind of relationship with Elijah. In doing so, Elisha ministered in a unique way to this old prophet. For three and a half years Elijah had carried the burden God had laid on his shoulders virtually by himself. For a full year he was literally alone as he hid from Ahab in the valley of Kerith.

Loneliness in itself causes depression, no doubt a basic factor in Elijah's difficult experience. True, with the exception of his year in isolation, he was often around other people. But they were not his friends.

I remember well the summers I spent in New York City working on my doctorate at New York University. Because we could not afford what it would cost to take my family with me, I had to leave Elaine and the children at home—at that time in Wheaton, Illinois.

How well I remember the lonely days and nights I spent without my family and other close friends. Weekends were the worst. I remember one Sunday afternoon particularly walking through Washington Square Park. People were everywhere—talking, laughing, playing games and enjoying other assorted activities with one another. Though I was in the midst of a crowd, I never felt so all alone! For one thing, my best friend—my wife Elaine—was a thousand miles away. It was indeed depressing.

Elijah needed a friend and Elisha became that friend! And, furthermore, he became a man with whom Elijah could share the deepest and most intimate details of his life without fear of rejection, misinterpretation, or betrayal. I'm personally convinced this was a very important factor in God's plan for delivering Elijah from his depressed state.

Elisha was always loyal to Elijah—a true test of friendship. Knowing the time was soon coming when they would be "temporarily" separated, Elisha would not leave his friend, even when Elijah asked him to stay behind. "I will not leave you" Elisha responded. And, "so the two of them walked on" *together* (2:6). And so it is with friends. They are loyal to each other and they "walk on" together no matter what the difficulties and problems in life.

Rosalie Carter captured the essence of this kind of friendship when she wrote:

I think that God will never send,
A gift so precious as a friend.
A friend who always understands,
And fills each need as it demands.
Whose loyalty will stand the test,
When skies are bright or overcast.
Who sees the faults that merit blame,
But keeps on loving just the same.
Who does far more than creeds could do,
To make us good, to make us true.
Earth's gifts a sweet contentment lend,
But only God can give a friend!

A TRUE DISCIPLE
2 Kings 2:7-14

There is yet another dimension to this relationship that must have encouraged Elijah greatly, helping him to forget his feelings of disillusionment and despair. Elisha became a *true disciple,* eager to learn everything he could from his friend and mentor. He wanted to be prepared to carry on Elijah's prophetic ministry when their separation came.

There are a couple of statements in this passage (2 Kings 2:7-14) that point to Elisha's desire to be a good learner.

First, he knew he could never take over Elijah's powerful position in Israel without supernatural help. Consequently, when Elijah asked his friend what he could do for him before he was taken from him, Elisha responded, "Let me inherit a double portion of your spirit" (2:9). Put another way, he was asking not that he be twice as successful as Elijah but that he be doubly blessed so he could measure up to Elijah's accomplishments. He felt he would need twice the motivation and faith that Elijah had, *just* to keep up with his friend's level of achievement in God's kingdom.

This then was not a selfish request uttered so that Elisha could rise to stardom and become bigger and greater than Elijah. He knew he could never fill this man's shoes. Just to keep up with Elijah, he knew he would need a "double portion" of his spirit. And seemingly because of his commitment to learn all he could from Elijah, his request was granted.

The second clue as to Elisha's "discipleship" relationship to Elijah comes into focus at the moment of separation. As Elijah disappeared into heaven in a whirlwind, separated from his friend by a "chariot of fire and horses of fire," Elisha cried out, *"My father! My father!"* (2:11-12).

Elisha viewed Elijah not as his "brother" but as his "father." In God's sight, they *were* brothers. In God's sight they were positionally equal—from a spiritual perspective.

But from a human point of view they were not equals. They were separated by age and experience. Elisha was like a son who looked to his father for guidance and help. He was a true disciple.

This was the kind of relationship that existed between Paul and Timothy in the New Testament. In fact, the parallels are uncanny. Paul called young Timothy to join him as his fellow missionary—in a sense to become his attendant (Acts 16:1-5). In the process they developed a very deep friendship, based on mutual trust and confidence. Paul captured the nature of this relationship in his letter to the Philippians. Writing from a Roman prison, he said: "I hope in the Lord Jesus to send Timothy to you soon, that I also may be cheered when I receive news about you. I have no one else like him, who takes a genuine interest in your welfare. For everyone looks out for his own interests, not those of Jesus Christ. But you know that Timothy has proved himself, because as *a son with his father* he has served with me in the work of the gospel" (Phil. 2:19-22).

Paul's discipleship relationship to Timothy is seen in his final letter to this man. In fact, it was the last letter he ever wrote before God took him home to heaven. Again, writing from prison, he said: "You then, *my son,* be strong in the grace that is in Christ Jesus. And the things you have heard me say in the presence of many witnesses entrust to reliable men who will also be qualified to teach others" (2 Tim. 2:1-2).

One of Paul's greatest sources of encouragement as he faced the prospect of death was to know that when he finished his work on earth it would go on through Timothy—his faithful attendant, his loyal friend, and his true disciple.

How much the same kind of relationship must have encouraged Elijah. Not that he needed someone to look up to him! Rather, he knew he was going to leave the work in the hands of a faithful man who had learned everything he could while they served together while on this earth and who would carry on the work successfully. This certainly must have been a key factor in helping Elijah overcome his bout with depression.

WHAT ABOUT YOU?

The relationship that existed between Elijah and Elisha yields a number of points of application. But the essence of that relationship can be summarized with one major point— *friendship*. All human beings need friends, those we can relate to at a deeper level than those who are mere acquaintances. It is a God-created means for helping us maintain our emotional equilibrium.

Following are some biblical principles and guidelines for developing and maintaining friendships.

1. God designed the husband and wife relationship to be a *friendship*. One of the most beautiful statements any marital partner can make about the other is to say, "This is my best friend." Unfortunately, many couples live together, but they are not close friends.

This is indeed a challenge for every Christian couple. God wants us to become friends—close friends—two people who can share their lives together in a total sense, becoming one not only physically, but emotionally and spiritually. Obviously this is a process that takes time and effort.

This point of application also speaks to those contemplating matrimony. Too many couples enter marriage without first becoming friends. The relationship is often built more on physical and emotional attraction rather than on a growing relationship that reflects true friendship.

Fortunately, couples can become friends after marriage. It is never too late. But, those who become friends *before* they take the final step have a decided head start in developing the kind of relationship God intended.[1]

2. Every couple needs friends outside of marriage.

Our children can and should become our best friends.

This is, of course, a process and usually does not happen until our children get beyond the teen years. One of the most exciting things I heard one of my grown daughters say one day was that she considered her mother her *best friend*! That one statement alone made the previous twenty years worth it all!

Every couple needs a close friendship with at least one other couple—and good friendships with several others.

If this is going to happen, every couple must take the initiative by being friendly. But remember, this takes time. People who do not respond may already have close friends. Furthermore, they may not be convinced they need close friends, even though they do. Also, people may not respond because of our own immaturity. We may be possessive. We may be trying too hard. In the process we scare people.

On the other hand, some people who desperately need friends sometimes withdraw and give the impression they don't want friends! And sure enough, they don't find them because people misinterpret their reactions.

Every husband needs a close *male friend and other* good *female friends outside of the marital relationship; and every wife needs a* close *female friend and other* good *male friends outside of the marriage.*

At this point we must be cautious. It is dangerous for a husband to have a *close* female friend other than his wife; and it's dangerous for a wife to have a *close* male friend who is not her husband. There are some who advocate this approach. It is lethal! Eventually, it can destroy a marriage.

On the other hand, every husband needs *good* female friendships; and every wife needs *good* male friendships. This is normal, natural, and necessary. And one way for a marriage to be destroyed is for a wife to be jealous of her husband's female friendships and for a husband to be jealous of his wife's male friendships. However, if either partner develops *close* friendships with the opposite sex, either partner has a right to be concerned.

3. Every unmarried person needs a close friend—hopefully more than one. Again, some cautions!

Opposite sex friendships by unmarried people can easily lead to illegitimate sexual expression. This is particularly true in a society that has adopted a value system that contradicts the Bible. God says that sex outside of marriage is sin. If we ignore God's laws, it will eventually lead to heartache, disillusionment, and God's discipline.

Friendships among unmarried people, though legitimate, can become possessive and exclusive. If they do it can easily destroy the friendship. This principle, of course, also applies to every relationship described thus far.

4. All Christians are friends because of our unique relationship in Christ.

True, we may not know a lot of other people well, but we have a common bond that goes beyond the dimensions of friendship that have just been described. Our relationships with one another are more than flesh and blood, feelings and emotions, and time spent with one another. We are friends because of our oneness in Jesus Christ.

I have felt this keenly in my opportunities to minister to Christians in other parts of the world. I have met total strangers, spent only a few hours together in spiritual communion, and when leaving I felt I had known these people for years. Very quickly our hearts were bound together in love. Why? Because of our spiritual relationship. We were brothers and sisters in Christ.

SOME CLOSING THOUGHTS

• "Some people make enemies instead of friends because it is less trouble." *E. C. McKenzie*

• "Be slow in choosing a friend, slower in changing." *Benjamin Franklin*

• "An old friend is better than two new ones." *Russian Proverb*

- "Associate yourself with men of good quality if you esteem your own reputation: for 'tis better to be alone than in bad company." *George Washington*
- "When we lose a friend we die a little."
- "If you really want to know who your friends are, just make a mistake." *The Bible Friend*
- "So long as we love we serve. No man is useless while he is a friend." *Robert Louis Stevenson*

Tribute to Friendship

I love you not only for what you are,
    but for what I am when I am with you;
I love you not only for what you have made of yourself,
    but for what you are making of me;
I love you not for closing your ears to the discords in me,
    but for adding to the music in me by worshipful listening;
You have done it without a touch, without a word, without a sign.
    You have done it just by being yourself.
Perhaps that is what being a friend means, after all.
Author Unknown

Note

1. To deepen your marital friendship, it is recommended that you study together the *Measure of a Marriage*, another Regal publication written by Gene Getz. A special workbook is also available and is essential to get maximum benefit from this study.

12

Life in Perspective

Elijah stands out in biblical history as one of the most significant Old Testament prophets who ever lived. Why was he so uniquely used by God? What was the secret of his success?

The facts are, it is no secret. The reasons why God used him so dramatically stand out in the story of his life as clearly as three mountain peaks silhouetted against the evening sky. As the sun sets on this old prophet's life, we can look back and see three primary reasons why God used Elijah to accomplish His purposes in this world.

ELIJAH WAS A MAN OF GOD

James stated that Elijah "was a man just like us," and the story of his life certainly verifies that reality. At times he was discouraged and lonely. At other times he was anxious and intensely fearful and disillusioned. He experienced the depth of depression—so much so that he wanted to die. But, in spite of his humanness, he was a "man of God."

That is an encouraging combination. In spite of human weaknesses and failures, God still uses men and women to do His work in this world. Elijah's life and witness certainly testify to that fact.

What factors in Elijah's life identify him as a man of God? There are several, but two stand out specifically.

God's Power Was Reveled Through His Life

Elijah was a *prophet of God,* who was unusually endowed with the *power of God.* Because of his unique calling, he was often identified as a *man of God.* For example, after he had prayed for the widow's son who had died, and had presented the boy alive, she responded, "Now I know that you are a *man of God*" (1 Kings 17:24). There was a clear cause/effect relationship between Elijah's ability to unleash God's supernatural power and the title the widow gave him.

Toward the end of his life, Elijah's reputation had spread far and wide. This is clearly illustrated by Ahaziah, who succeeded his father Ahab as king of Israel. On one occasion he injured himself badly and sent messengers to consult a false god to try to discover if he was going to recover. However the Lord revealed to Elijah what Ahaziah was about to do and sent him to meet the messengers with a prophetic pronouncement. "Is it because there is no God in Israel that you are going off to consult Baal-Zebub, the god of Ekron?" Elijah asked. "Therefore, this is what the Lord says: 'You will not leave the bed you are lying on. You will certainly die' " (2 Kings 1:3-4).

Ahaziah's messengers returned to the king and reported what they had heard. It appears that this kind of report was very familiar to the king, which prompted a question. "What *kind of man* was it who came to meet you and told you this?" he asked (1:7).

Not knowing who Elijah was, the messengers identified him by his appearance, "He was a man with a garment of hair and a leather belt around his waist." Immediately the king knew who had sent the message. "That was Elijah the Tishbite," the king responded (1:8).

King Ahaziah made this positive identification for two reasons. First, because of Elijah's appearance. But second, and most important, because of his reputation as a "man of God" (1:9). And that reputation was directly associated with Elijah's relationship with God, particularly in being able to unleash God's power in miraculous ways. His reputation had preceded him in the eyes of King Ahaziah.

That cause/effect relationship is seen when the messengers approached Elijah with the message from Ahaziah actually identifying him as a *man of God*. "If I am a *man of God*," Elijah responded, "may fire come down from heaven and consume you and your fifty men!" Sure enough, fire fell, verifying Elijah's unique relationship with God (1:12).

Elijah's Unequivocal Statements Regarding His Relationship with God

Elijah demonstrated who he was not only by *what he did*, but also by *what he said*. He made it clear that there was only one God in his life—the God of Abraham, Isaac and Jacob. When he first confronted Ahab regarding his sins of idolatry, Elijah let it be known immediately that he *served the living God* (1 Kings 17:1)—not idols of wood and stone. And three and a half years later, when conversing with his friend Obadiah, he made this unequivocal statement, "As the Lord Almighty lives, *whom I serve,* I will surely present myself to Ahab today" (1 Kings 18:15).

There was no question in people's minds who knew Elijah, either personally or by reputation, whom he served. God was first in his life. Beyond anything else he wanted to honor God's name. He was so committed to the Lord he was willing to put his own life on the line. He would not compromise his convictions either in worship or in his lifestyle. He was a "man of God."

A MAN OF PRAYER

Elijah's reputation as a "man of God" was also clearly associated with his prayer life. In fact, this is the aspect of his life that impressed James. Though he "was a man just like us," James wrote, yet, "he *prayed earnestly* that it would not rain . . . . Again he *prayed,* and the heavens gave rain, and the earth produced its crops" (Jas. 5:17-18).

Every major miracle associated with Elijah's life is also associated with prayer. As we've just seen from James's statement, the three-and-a-half-year drought began and ended when Elijah prayed. The widow's son was healed when he cried out for healing (1 Kings 17:17-23). And fire fell on Mount Carmel when he "stepped forward and prayed" (18:36-37).

The connection is clear: "Man of God—man of prayer!"

The greatest lesson we can learn from Elijah's prayer life focuses on his primary motives. When he prayed that it might not rain, it was to demonstrate to Israel that there was only one true God (17:1). When he prayed that fire might fall from heaven to consume the sacrifice, again it was to demonstrate to Israel who God was—but also who he, Elijah, was. "Let it be known today *that you are God* in Israel and that *I am your servant* and have done all these things at *your* command" (18:36). In other words, Elijah's motives in prayer were to let Israel know that it was *God*—the one true God—who answers prayer and demonstrates power; and that he, Elijah, was just a *servant* of God, carrying out the Lord's orders. Though a man of God, he wanted everyone to know he was a *servant* of God. That, indeed, is the essence of true commitment.

A MAN OF GOD'S WORD

More is said about Elijah's obedience to God than any other factor. There is a unique pattern that is repeated again and again. *First,* God revealed His will to Elijah. *Second,* Elijah obeyed!

God's revelation regarding the ravine of Kerith
> 1 Kings17:2—"Then the word of the Lord came to Elijah"
>> 17:5—"So he did what the Lord had told him."

God's revelation regarding the widow in Sidon
>> 17:8—"Then the word of the Lord came to him"
>> 17:10—"So he went."

God's revelation regarding Elijah's confrontation with Ahab
>> 18:1—"The word of the Lord came to Elijah"
>> 18:2—"So Elijah went."

God's revelation regarding the call of Elisha
>> 19:15—"The Lord said to him"
>> 19:19—"So Elijah went."

God's revelation regarding the messengers of King Ahaziah
> 2 Kings 1:3—"But the angel of the Lord said to Elijah"
>> 1:4—"So Elijah went."

God's revelation regarding Elijah's confrontation with King Ahaziah
>> 1:15a—"The angel of the Lord said to Elijah"
>> 1:15b—"So Elijah got up and went."

The pattern is clear. Each time God told Elijah to do something, he responded. Though he went through a time of deep depression that temporarily affected his ability to respond to the Lord, eventually he obeyed God's voice and once again experienced God's power and blessing in his life.

ELIJAH AND EVERY TWENTIETH-CENTURY CHRISTIAN

Elijah's "life in perspective" leads to some very practical questions. When you and I come to the end of our lives on earth, what will people remember about us? That is a very thought-provoking and convicting question, one that I wrestled with personally as I wrote this chapter. What will my children remember? What will my friends remember? What will my associates remember? What will those I've ministered to remember about my life?

Just so, every Christian should ask the same questions. What will people remember about *you* when your sojourn in this life is over? Will they remember:

- Your success as a Christian parent
- Your commitment to your church
- Your business acumen
- Your wealth
- Your unselfish spirit
- Your concern for others
- Your soul winning efforts
- Your teaching and preaching ability
- Your diligence
- Your family
- Your organizational ability
- Your loving spirit
- Your patience
- Your faith
- Your knowledge of the Bible
- Your benevolence?

Certainly all of these factors are significant, noteworthy and even praiseworthy! But is there something *more* significant and *more* noteworthy and *more* praiseworthy? I think there is.

As we've seen in this study, there are many lessons we can learn from Elijah's life and ministry. But beyond anything else is what characterized this "man just like us" and what we remember most about his life. For those who come to know him well there is only one conclusion. He was a *man of God*, a *man of prayer*, and a *man committed to obeying God's Word*. That combination of factors tells us clearly why God used him so significantly and why he stands tall in biblical history as one of the greatest prophets who ever lived.

Elijah emerges then as an example for every twentieth-century Christian. Is it possible to be remembered in the same way? The answer is yes *if* we develop Elijah's perspective on life. True, he was a unique person, especially called and empowered by God.

- As a *man of God,* he was one of those special people who had access to God's power to work miracles.
- As a *man of prayer,* he was one of those unique people who saw God respond in very unusual ways.
- As a *man of God's Word,* he heard God speak to him directly on numerous occasions, revealing His specific will!

However, this unique calling, this unique power, this unique access to God does not mean we cannot be remembered in the same way.

- We too can be men and women of God—people reflecting our commitment to God and demonstrating His character and power in our lives.
- We too can be men and women of prayer, seeing God answer in unusual ways. As James reminded some first-century Christians, "You do not have, because you do not ask God. When you ask, you do not receive, because you ask with wrong motives, that you may spend what you get on your pleasures" (Jas. 4:2b,3).
- We too can hear God's voice, clearly and precisely, as He has spoken through Scripture. And we can choose to obey or disobey what He has said.

How then will people remember you—and me?

Dr. William Culberson served as president of Moody Bible Institute for many years. When he died, Warren Wiersbe was asked to write the official biography of his life. After talking at length with his family and his close associates, after reading through his correspondence and a number of his sermons, and after completing the manuscript telling the story of his life, the author chose the title for the book. Interestingly, and not surprisingly, it was *William*

Culberson—A Man of God. The late Dr. Wilbur Smith said of Dr. Culberson, "My first impression and a lasting one is that he is a *man of God*."

In my thirteen years as a faculty member of Moody Bible Institute I got to know Dr. Culberson quite well—in some respects better than others did. And when I explain, you'll understand why. You see, we played nearly ten years of volleyball together, sometimes two or three times a week. About half the time I played on his team. At other times, we were fierce competitors, playing opposite each other. When we played together, since I was considerably younger, I spiked and he set up the ball. Incidentally, he was one of the best set-up men I've ever worked with.

Following our workout, we often talked at length in the shower room, since his locker was next to mine. A lot of conversation involved just good-natured kidding and ribbing. At times it was very serious. As anyone knows who is involved in sports, it's at times like these that you really get to know people. What we really *are* comes out under pressure. In this setting I felt I got to know the real Dr. Culberson.

When the book was published telling the story of his life, those who knew him well were not surprised at the title! It was an accurate description. Though he was a man just like any one of us—and I saw that often on the volleyball court, I never saw him violate his spiritual convictions. And if he thought he did, he was always quick to right the wrong!

Perhaps this is why I remember something he said in chapel one day, as if he said it yesterday. I was seated with the faculty, just really beginning my teaching career at that time. Speaking with deep conviction, he said to the students as he gestured toward those of us seated in the faculty section, "Young people, you will forget what these teachers *say*, but you will never forget what they *are*!"

The message was directed at the students! But the

impact hit me, and I'm sure my fellow faculty members as well. And the statement became even more meaningful against the backdrop of his life.

How true his statement was. And is this not what we remember about Elijah? Is this not what stands out in the record of his life? It was what he *was as a man of God* that highlights his life. What he *said* only reflected his relationship with the God he served!

During his lifetime, Jonathan Edwards, that great preacher and teacher, set forth these five resolutions for his life:

"Resolve, to live with all my might while I do live.

"Resolve, never to lose one moment of time, to improve it in the most profitable way I can.

"Resolve, never to do anything which I should despise or think meanly of in another.

"Resolve, never to do anything out of revenge.

"Resolve, never to do anything which I should be afraid if it were the last hour of my life."

THREE RESOLUTIONS

There are many valid ways to set forth spiritual convictions and resolutions for our lives. But Elijah's example gives us three of the most basic resolutions that reflect God's will for every Christian:

- Resolve, to always be a *man or woman of God*—putting Him first in all I do, never bringing His name and reputation into disrepute, and by God's grace, to always reflect His righteousness.
- Resolve, to be a *man or woman of prayer,* never attempting to achieve goals in my own strength alone, but always seeking His guidance, His enabling, His divine assistance and help. And when He does answer, to always give God the glory due His name.
- Resolve, to be a *man or woman of God's Word,* consistently learning more of what God says, interpreting it

accurately, and always obeying the Lord's spiritual direc-
tives and consistently applying His divine principles.

Would you read these resolutions again—and make
them *your* resolutions?

Center for Church Renewal

The local church is God's primary social unit in the world ... however, the church includes smaller interrelated units: the family, the marriage and the individual.

Biblical Renewal

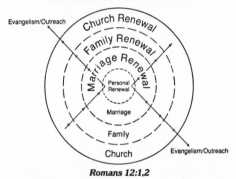

Romans 12:1,2

Can you identify where the greatest need is in the Christian community today:

> in the church?
> in the family?
> in marriage?
> in personal Christian living?

The Center for Church Renewal exists to help bring biblical renewal to every segment of the Christian community.

For more information, write:
> Center for Church Renewal
> Box 863173
> Plano, TX 75086